Frommer's

Beijing
day BY day™

2nd Edition

by Jen Lin-Liu

WILEY

Wiley Publishing, Inc.

Contents

Published by:

Wiley Publishing, Inc.

111 River St.
Hoboken, NJ 07030-5774

ISBN 978-0-470-63006-8 (paper); 978-0-470-92888-2 (ebk);
978-0-470-92889-9 (ebk); 978-0-470-92890-5 (ebk).
Editor: Ian Skinnari
Production Editor: Eric T. Schroeder
Photo Editor: Richard Fox
Cartographer: Roberta Stockwell
Production by Wiley Indianapolis Composition Services

For information on our other products and services or to obtain technical support, please contact our Customer Care Department within the U.S. at 877/762-2974, outside the U.S. at 317/572-3993 or fax 317/572-4002.

Wiley also publishes its books in a variety of electronic formats. Some content that appears in print may not be available in electronic formats.

Manufactured in China

5   4   3   2   1

A Note from the Editorial Director

Organizing your time. That's what this guide is all about.

Other guides give you long lists of things to see and do and then expect you to fit the pieces together. The Day by Day guides are different. These guides tell you the best of everything, and then they show you how to see it *in the smartest, most time-efficient way.* Our authors have designed detailed itineraries organized by time, neighborhood, or special interest. And each tour comes with a bulleted map that takes you from stop to stop.

Hoping to climb the Great Wall, or to explore the Forbidden City? Planning to visit Tian'anmen Square, ride a bicycle through Beijing's hutongs, or roam the courtyards of Lama Temple? Whatever your interest or schedule, the Day by Days give you the smartest route to follow. Not only do we take you to the top sights and attractions, but we introduce you to those special moments that only locals know about—those "finds" that turn tourists into travelers.

The Day by Days are also your top choice if you're looking for one complete guide for all your travel needs. The best hotels and restaurants for every budget, the greatest shopping values, the wildest nightlife—it's all here.

Why should you trust our judgment? Because our authors personally visit each place they write about. They're an independent lot who say what they think and would never include places they wouldn't recommend to their best friends. They're also open to suggestions from readers. If you'd like to contact them, please send your comments our way at feedback@frommers.com, and we'll pass them on.

Enjoy your Day by Day guide—the most helpful travel companion you can buy. And have the trip of a lifetime.

Warm regards,

Kelly Regan

Kelly Regan, Editorial Director
Frommer's Travel Guides

About the Author

Jen Lin-Liu is a food and culture writer and the owner of the Beijing cooking school Black Sesame Kitchen. Most recently, she is the author of *Serve the People: A Stir-Fried Journey Through China* (Harcourt, 2008), which received wide praise from publications ranging from *The New York Review of Books* to *People*. A former correspondent for *Newsweek* in Shanghai, she is a regular food and arts contributor for *The New York Times*. She has authored several *Frommer's* travel guides in Asia and has written for *The Wall Street Journal, Saveur, Food & Wine,* and *Travel + Leisure*. She first went to China in 2000 on a Fulbright fellowship, after growing up in southern California and graduating from Columbia University. Learn more about her work at jenlinliu.com.

Acknowledgments

Jen Lin-Liu would like to thank Candice Lee for her help in creating this book, as well as Sherisse Pham for her work on the previous edition. She is also grateful to her husband, Craig, for his unwavering support, assistance researching the nooks and crannies of Beijing, and for his photographs that grace the pages of this book.

An Additional Note

Please be advised that travel information is subject to change at any time—and this is especially true of prices. We therefore suggest that you write or call ahead for confirmation when making your travel plans. The authors, editors, and publisher cannot be held responsible for the experiences of readers while traveling. Your safety is important to us, however, so we encourage you to stay alert and be aware of your surroundings.

Star Ratings, Icons & Abbreviations

Every hotel, restaurant, and attraction listing in this guide has been ranked for quality, value, service, amenities, and special features using a **star-rating system.** Hotels, restaurants, attractions, shopping, and nightlife are rated on a scale of zero stars (recommended) to three stars (exceptional). In addition to the star-rating system, we also use a **kids icon** to point out the best bets for families. Within each tour, we recommend cafes, bars, or restaurants where you can take a break. Each of these stops appears in a shaded box marked with a coffee-cup-shaped bullet ☕

The following **abbreviations** are used for credit cards:

AE	American Express	DISC	Discover	V	Visa
DC	Diners Club	MC	MasterCard		

Travel Resources at Frommers.com

Frommer's travel resources don't end with this guide. Frommer's website, **www.frommers.com**, has travel information on more than 4,000 destinations. We update features regularly, giving you access to the most current trip-planning information and the best airfare, lodging, and car-rental bargains. You can also listen to podcasts, connect with other Frommers.com members through our active-reader forums, share your travel photos, read blogs from guidebook editors and fellow travelers, and much more.

A Note on Prices

In the "Take a Break" and "Best Bets" sections of this book, we have used a system of dollar signs to show a range of costs for 1 night in a hotel (the price of a double-occupancy room) or the cost of an entree at a restaurant. Use the following table to decipher the dollar signs:

Cost	Hotels	Restaurants
$	under $65	under $10
$$	$65–$130	$10–$15
$$$	$130–$260	$15–$25
$$$$	$260–$390	$25–$40
$$$$$	over $390	over $40

How to Contact Us

In researching this book, we discovered many wonderful places—hotels, restaurants, shops, and more. We're sure you'll find others. Please tell us about them, so we can share the information with your fellow travelers in upcoming editions. If you were disappointed with a recommendation, we'd love to know that, too. Please write to:

Frommer's Beijing, Day by Day, 2nd Edition
Wiley Publishing, Inc. • 111 River St. • Hoboken, NJ 07030-5774

13 Favorite **Moments**

13 Favorite **Moments**

Map labels: Xihai, Houhai, Jiugulou Dajie, Gulou Xi Dajie, Houhai Nanyan 后海南沿, Gulou Dongdajie, Jiaodaokou, Andingmennei Dajie, Yonghegong Dajie, 雍和宫大街, Deshengmennei Dajie, Qianhai, 地安门西大街 Di'anmen Xi Dajie, 地安门东大街 Di'anmen Dong Dajie, Zhangzi Zhong Lu, Fuxue Hutong, Xinjiekou Nan Dajie, Xishiku Dajie, Beihai, DONGCHENG, 东四北大街 Dongsi Bei Dajie, Dongsi Xidajie, Dongsi Nan Dajie, Jingshan Park, Jingshan Qian Jie, Bei Chang Jie, FORBIDDEN CITY, Bei Heyan Dajie, Bei Chizi Dajie, Wangfujing Dajie 王府井大街, Zhongshan Park, Dong Chang'an Jie 东长安街, TIAN'ANMEN SQUARE, Qianmen Dajie, 前门东大街 Qianmen Dong Dajie, Qian Dajie, Chongwenmenwai Dajie, 珠市口东大街 Zhushikou Dong Dajie, Tiantan Lu 天坛路, Temple of Heaven Park, Bei Wei Lu, Nan Wei Lu

0 ___ 1 mi
0 ___ 1 km

Previous page: Walking the Simatai section of the Great Wall.

At first glimpse, Beijing isn't a conventionally attractive city. But look a little more closely and you can't help but be captivated by this city's contradictions and contrasts. Modern skyscrapers spring up in neighborhoods of traditional courtyard homes. Fancy fusion restaurants open up next to street-side snack stalls. Rolls-Royces speed past bicycles and, occasionally, donkey carts. Amid the chaos, the full-throttle rush into the future, here are some of our favorite moments. Savor them, and you'll come to love Beijing as we have.

The Great Wall.

1 Climb the Great Wall. Though it might sound like a cliché, the Great Wall is an absolute must. This ancient Chinese landmark meanders to dizzying heights. Avoid the crowds and tacky tourist traps by heading to an unrestored section. *See p 133.*

2 Eat Peking duck. In a town with few local specialties, this sumptuous dish stands out as a legacy of Beijing's imperial era. Be prepared for juicy duck meat and crisp skin wrapped around paper-thin pancakes flavored with a savory-sweet dark sauce. It's best experienced at either Da Dong or Made in China. *See p 81.*

3 Take a romantic walk around Houhai Lake. The late afternoon, just around sunset, is the best time to take a stroll around the lake. Tacky tourist touts give way to an idyllic scene of weeping willows brushing the shore while locals play chess or take a dip in waters of questionable cleanliness—all part of the charm. Walk to the western banks for optimum tranquillity. *See p 11.*

4 Go fly a kite. Join the locals in the square just behind the Drum Tower, in the heart of Beijing's old courtyard district. *See p 12.*

5 Browse the galleries at cutting-edge art districts. Beijing boasts one of the best art scenes in the world at the moment—visit the galleries at Caochangdi and 798 to see why. *See p 21.*

6 Spend an evening rocking out to live punk, indie, and metal at one of Beijing's thriving live music clubs. Check out the youth culture scene at Mao Livehouse or Yugong Yushan—what you see might

Rocking out at Mao Livehouse.

One of Beijing's many hutongs.

surprise you and defy your ideas of a Communist "party." *See p 101.*

7 Have a cocktail atop the roof at The Emperor. This new boutique hotel has a great view of the Forbidden City and its moat—it's the perfect place to unwind after a day of sightseeing. *See p 123.*

8 Ride a bicycle through the hutongs. You'll find yourself sitting bolt upright on an old-fashioned bike as you coast through the back alleys (hutongs) of Beijing. *See p 28.*

9 Escape for a weekend retreat at the Aman Beijing. This gorgeous new resort offers palatial rooms fit for emperors and VIP access to the Summer Palace. *See p 120.*

10 Shop 'til you drop. Everything is made in China these days—and yes, it's cheaper in China. For those looking for bargain designer threads, head to the Zoo Market and the Ritan Office Building. *See p 62.*

11 Gaze down at Tian'anmen Square from the top of the Forbidden City. From this spot, Chairman Mao made many of his announcements. Make sure to look for his mausoleum on the far end of Tian'anmen Square. *See p 8.*

12 Get a foot massage. A recent boom in spas in Beijing means there are more choices than ever to unwind—my favorite local spa is Bodhi, where bargain massages come with free drinks and food. *See p 46.*

13 Take a morning walk at Beihai Park. This enormous park contains a gorgeous lake and a white Buddhist stupa, but just as engrossing are the senior citizens doing tai chi and using gigantic brushes to scrawl Chinese calligraphy in water on the sidewalks. *See p 11.* ●

The Best **in One Day**

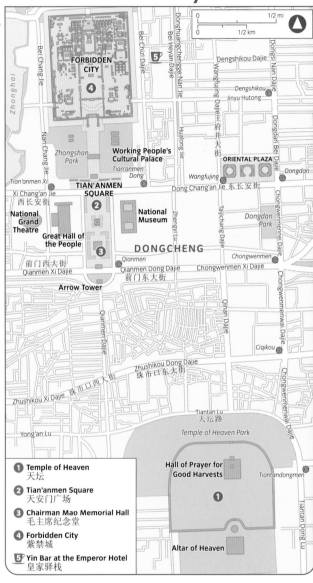

1 **Temple of Heaven**
天坛

2 **Tian'anmen Square**
天安门广场

3 **Chairman Mao Memorial Hall**
毛主席纪念堂

4 **Forbidden City**
紫禁城

5 **Yin Bar at the Emperor Hotel**
皇家驿栈

Previous page: The New Summer Palace.

If you have only 1 day in Beijing, be prepared to kick into cultural overdrive. We're going to take you to the major historical sites that played witness to some of China's most defining moments. The tour itself is a study in juxtapositions: You'll see an imperial palace, an ancient symbol of wealth and opulence, standing next to Beijing's infamous, starkly Communist-style structures. Each stop on the tour recalls a moment in China's long and varied past, and the frenzied activity swirling around you at every turn is a reminder that the city's entrance onto the international scene has just begun. START: **Temple of Heaven, west gate.**

Travel Tip

With the expansion of the Beijing metro system over the last few years, taking the subway has never been easier. Most destinations are within a few minutes' walk of a subway stop, and mass transit buffs will find one of the cheapest rides in the world, at ¥2 per ride. An added bonus is that you won't have to deal with Beijing's horrendous traffic. On the other hand, if you're traveling outside of rush hours (weekdays 8–10am and 4–7pm) and have the name of your destination written in Chinese (as most taxi drivers don't speak English), taxis—which are also inexpensive and plentiful—might be the way to go.

① ★ kids **Temple of Heaven (Tiantan Gongyuan).** Just after dawn, regular park goers practice tai chi, kung fu, group dancing, or giant calligraphy on this park's greenery and paved walkways. You'll probably hear birds and crickets chirping happily through their cages as their owners (mostly retired elderly men) take them out for a walk. The park is huge; don't miss ★★ **Qian Dian (Hall of Prayer for Good Harvests).** Although the building's origins date from 1420, the current structure is a replica built in 1889 after the original burned to the ground. The circular

wooden hall, with its triple-layered cylindrical blue-tiled roof, is perhaps the most recognizable emblem of Chinese imperial architecture outside of the Forbidden City. The main hall is 38m (125 ft.) high and 30m (98 ft.) in diameter and—here's the kicker—it was constructed without a single nail. ⏱ *1½ hr.; arrive at 7am to catch the morning buzz. 1 Tiantan Donglu Jia.* ☎ *010/6702-8866. Admission park only Apr–Oct ¥15; Nov–Mar ¥10. Access to all sites Apr–Oct ¥35; Nov–Mar ¥30. Park daily 6am–8pm (park closes 1 hr. earlier in the winter); sites daily 8am–4pm (sites close 30 min. earlier in winter). Metro: Tiantandongmen; exit station on the south side and take a ¥10 cab ride to the temple's east gate.*

② **Tian'anmen Square (Tian'anmen Guangchang).** Tian'anmen is a mere stripling

The Hall of Prayer for Good Harvests.

A side view of the Forbidden City, protected by a bronze lion.

compared to other Chinese emblems that date back many centuries. The square was built in the 1950s, after Mao cleared away all the old government ministries. Thankfully, cash ran out before he also realized plans to "press down" the "feudal" Forbidden City. ⏲ *30 min. It's best to take the subway or approach the square by foot, as taxis aren't allowed to stop in front. Located, literally, in the center of Beijing. Free admission. Metro stops: Tian'anmen East or Tian'anmen West.*

❸ Chairman Mao Memorial Hall (Mao Zhuxi Jinnian Tang).

I'm always surprised by how small Mao looks (official sources state that Mao was 180cm tall, or just under 5 ft. 11 in.). For a man who holds such an important place in history, it's odd to see him occupying so little physical space. Sure, there are more critical issues to think about when viewing Mao, but you're given very little time for reflection as you are quickly shuffled around the roped barrier. See "Keeping Up Appearances," p 25. ⏲ *20 min. South end of Tian'anmen Square Tues–Sun 8–11:30am, sometimes also 2–4pm (usually Tues, Thurs). Admission free. Bag storage across the street, directly west, for ¥3 per piece. Metro: Tian'anmen East or West. Walk toward the south-central end of Tian'anmen Square.*

❹ ★★ Forbidden City (Gu Gong).

The very name of this historic site induces goose bumps. You are entering a place that is so vast, so grand and impressive, that mere civilians were once denied access; this is Beijing's Buckingham Palace or Versailles.

5 Yin Bar at The Emperor Hotel. Sip a cocktail while watching the sun set behind the sparkling yellow roofs of the Forbidden City. *33 Qihelou St, Emperor Hotel.* ☎ *010/6526-5566. Open daily Apr–Oct 3:30pm–midnight. $$.*

Sculptures in front of the Chairman Mao Memorial Hall.

Forbidden City

Shenwu Gate

IMPERIAL GARDEN

Palace of Heavenly Purity

Qianqing Gate

Hall of Clocks

Hall of Paintings **4B**

4E

4D

4C

Palace of Earthly Tranquility

Hall of Preserving Harmony

4A

Palace Moat

Palace Moat

Hall of Middle Harmony

Hall of Great Harmony

Hongyi Pavilion

Tiren Pavilion

Imperial Library

Zhendu Gate

Zhaode Gate

Xihua Gate

Gate of Great Harmony

Donghua Gate

Some of the Forbidden City's most charming areas lie along its eastern axis. The ticket booth is south of Qianqing Men. After entering, walk straight to the **4A Nine Dragon Screen,** a glazed tile wall meant to protect the emperor from malevolent spirits. Directly opposite is the **4B Hall of Jewelry,** housing imperial seals and headpieces. Continue to the highlight of the area, **4C ★★ Ningshou Gong Huayuan.** This is where the Qianlong emperor (ruled 1735–96) was meant to spend his retirement. Water once filled the winding trough carved into the floor of the main pavilion. A cup of wine would be sent down the stream, and the person nearest to where it stopped would have to compose a poem or drink the wine. To the north is **4D ★★ Leshou Tang,** which houses a beautiful pavilion built entirely of sandalwood. In the final hall, Yihe Xuan, you'll find **4E Zhen**

Fei Jing (Well of the Pearl Concubine). The Pearl Concubine was one of the Guangxu emperor's (ruled 1875–1908) favorites. Empress Cixi had her thrown down this well as they were fleeing in the aftermath of the Boxer Rebellion. According to several accounts, the girl angered Cixi when she suggested Guangxu stay and face the foreign troops. ⏱ *3 hr. North side of Tian'anmen Square across Chang'an Dajie.* ☎ *010/6513-2255. Admission ¥60 Apr–Oct; ¥40 Nov–Mar. Metro: Tian'anmen West.*

A roof detail at the Forbidden City.

The Best **in Two Days**

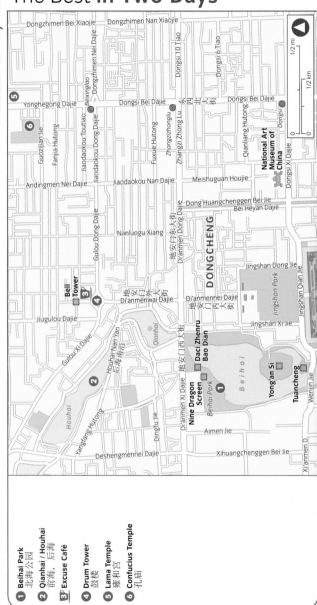

1 **Beihai Park**
北海公园

2 **Qianhai / Houhai**
前海，后海

3 **Excuse Café**

4 **Drum Tower**
鼓楼

5 **Lama Temple**
雍和宫

6 **Confucius Temple**
孔庙

If you have 2 days, spend your first day as detailed in "The Best in One Day" (p 6). On your second day, we'll show you Beijing's more playful side, such as the summer palaces that once served as pleasure grounds for the ruling class and the lakes where Mao took leisurely swims. As you visit the stops on this tour, you'll probably notice that the locals are moving at a less frenzied pace than their downtown counterparts. START: **South entrance of Beihai Park.**

❶ ★ Beihai Park (Beihai Gongyuan). Set around a lake dug in the 12th century, Beihai Park first began to serve as an imperial summer playground during the Jin dynasty. The Yuan dynasty's (1206–1368) imperial palace once stood on the eastern shore of Beihai; today its sole remnant is **Tuancheng** (Circular City, or "the smallest city of China"), a small citadel on a raised platform whose most notable structure, **Chengguang Dian**, houses a 1.5m (5-ft.) statue of Buddha crafted from Burmese white jade. Also housed in Tuancheng is a massive jade urn that once held Kublai Khan's wine. North of Tuancheng (across the bridge) is the white, flask-shaped *dagoba* (a structure built over Buddhist relics), visible from various high points in Beijing. A steep climb through **Yong'an Si** (Temple of Eternal Peace) leads to the *dagoba*. The temple buildings contain statues of Buddhas, bodhisattvas, and Panchen and Dalai Lamas. Many of the paths down the other side of the hill lead to dead ends so it's best to return the way you came and head back to the bridge. You can wander to the north shore by foot or row yourself across the lake by boat. A stand just west of the bridge rents battery-operated motorboats, pedal boats, and rowboats, but only rowboats can be returned at stands on the other side of the lake (other boats have to be returned to the place of rental). A five-person rowboat is ¥30 per hour plus a ¥200 deposit. On the north

The Nine Dragon Screen in Beihai Park.

shore, you will find the **Daci Zhenru Bao Dian,** a Ming dynasty hall housing three huge statues of Sakyamuni, the Amithaba Buddha and Yaoshi Fo. Nearby, the **Nine Dragon Screen** is a magnificent stretch of colored glaze tile that once guarded the entrance of a now-vanished temple. Continue east to the park's north gate and exit onto Ping'an Dadao. 🕐 *2–3 hr.; best before 10am. Beihai Park's south entrance is just west of the north gate of the Forbidden City at Wenjin Jie 1, Xi1 Cheng Qu.* ☎ *010/6404-0610. Admission ¥10 Apr–Oct; ¥5 Nov–Mar; ¥10 additional for entrance to the dagoba. Metro: Zhangzizhonglu.*

❷ ★★ kids Qianhai/Houhai (The Lake District). Qianhai and Houhai's banks, now overflowing with alfresco bars, cafes, and the odd curio shop, were once exclusive areas for nobles and merchants.

Boating on Houhai Lake.

Prior to 1911, only people with connections to the imperial family were permitted to maintain houses and conduct business here. The present-day commercial fare on the main banks can be wearying, but the area's back alleys are still ripe for exploration. Walk northeast along Qianhai Nanyan until you come to Yinding Qiao (Silver Ingot Bridge), the bridge that marks the boundary between Qianhai and Houhai. From here you can watch the boats drifting along below, several of which have zither players strumming classics such as "Moon River" for foreign passengers. If you want your own Sino-Western serenade, you can rent boats from the small dock

A performance at the Drum Tower.

near the Lotus Lane entrance. 🕐 *1½ hr. Di'anmenwai Dajie, enter near Lotus Lane and turn right. Free admission. If you are coming from Beihai's north gate, the entrance to Qianhai is across the street.*

3 ★ **Excuse Café.** Just east of the back entrance of the Drum Tower is this cozy cafe serving excellent espressos. *68 Zhonglou Wan Hutong.* ☎ *010/6401-9867. $.*

4 **Drum Tower (Gu Lou).** We recommend climbing only one tower's set of steep stairs, preferably those of the Drum Tower. The upper chamber has replicas of traditional drums, which are showcased in performances several times per hour. Outside, if it's a clear day, you'll see fantastic views of Houhai Lake to the west. 🕐 *½ hr. 9 Zhonglouwan Linzi. Admission ¥20. Walk northeast from Yinding Qiao and turn right at Moscow restaurant, onto Yandai Xiejie. Walk to the end of this alley until you come to the main street, Di'anmenwai Dajie. The Drum Tower is directly north, or to your left.*

5 ★ **Lama Temple (Yonghe-gong).** Though often referred to as the Lama Temple, Yonghegong means "The Palace of Peace and Harmony." On a quiet day, you can roam around the many courtyards at a leisurely pace, exploring the temple's impressive offerings, such as a 6m (20-ft.) bronze statue of Tsongkapa (1357–1419), founder of the now dominant school of Tibetan Buddhism, housed in **Falun Dian (Hall of the Wheel of Law).** You'll find the temple's most prized possession in the last of the major halls, **Wanfu Ge (Tower of Ten Thousand Happiness).** There, standing 18m (59 ft.) tall, is the Tibetan-style statue of Maitreya (the future Buddha), carved from a single piece of white sandalwood and transported all the way from Tibet as a gift to Qianlong from the seventh Dalai Lama. ⏱ *1 hr. To avoid crowds, delay lunch and tour the site noon–1pm. 12 Yonghegong Dajie (entrance on the south side of the complex).* ☎ *010/6404-4499. Admission ¥25. Nov–Mar 9am–4pm; Apr–Oct 9am–4:30pm. Metro: Yonghegong.*

Statue of Confucius.

❻ **Confucius Temple (Kong Miao).** On a tree-shaded street west of Yonghegong, you'll come to China's second largest Confucius Temple. Two stelae at the front instruct you, in six different languages, to park your horse (in Chinese: *Xia ma bei,* "Please Dismount"). The temple is the busiest before national university entrance examinations, when students and parents descend in droves to seek out the Great Sage's assistance. The main hall, **Dacheng Dian,** is the focal point for students, who must throw their incense on the shrine rather than burn it because of fire regulations. ⏱ *20 min. 13 Guo Zi Jian.* ☎ *010/6404-2407. Admission ¥10. Metro: Yonghegong. Walk across the street from the Lama Temple, heading to the west side of Yonghegong Dajie. Turn right into a street marked with an arch.*

The Major Lamas

Via the Silk Route, Buddhism reached China during the first century. Over the years, it has been denounced as a barbarian religion and banned. Lamaism, or Tibetan Buddhism, began to dominate other forms of Buddhism in China with the arrival of the Manchu Qing in 1644. Founded by Tsongkapa (see ❺, above), Tibetan Buddhism's key lamas (enlightened senior monks who have passed qualifications) are the 14th Dalai Lama, who lives in forced exile in India, and the Panchen Lama, whose current reincarnation, Dedhun Choekyi Nyima, was only 6 years old when the Dalai Lama recognized him, in 1995, prompting his arrest by the Chinese government. He is known as the world's youngest political prisoner.

The Best **in Three Days**

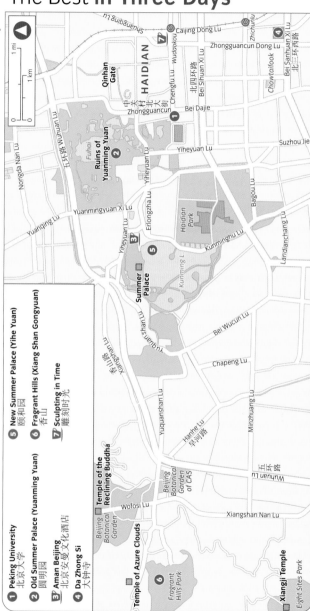

1 Peking University
北京大学

2 Old Summer Palace (Yuanming Yuan)
圆明园

3 Aman Beijing
北京安曼文化酒店

4 Da Zhong Si
大钟寺

5 New Summer Palace (Yihe Yuan)
颐和园

6 Fragrant Hills (Xiang Shan Gongyuan)
香山

7 Sculpting in Time
雕刻时光

After touring the central sites covered in "The Best in Two Days," it's time to get away from the city's core. The third full-day tour ventures into the far northwest corner of Beijing. This district is home to China's top two universities, the self-styled Harvard and MIT of China, as well as the Beijing Foreign Language and Culture University (BLCU), where you can find foreign students from all over the world learning Chinese. Nestled among all the student bars, Wi-Fi cafes, and intellectual activity, are a couple of imperial palaces. START: **East gate of Peking University.**

❶ Peking University (Beijing Daxue or "Beida"). China's most famous university, commonly known as Beida, has traditionally housed student activists, including some of the leaders of the infamous Tian'anmen demonstrations of 1989 (ironically, the campus has a road called Minzhu Lu, Democracy Road). You can ponder the campus' historical significance from the rocky seats surrounding **Weiminghu (Weiming Lake).** Better yet, if you are visiting in winter, rent some skates and take a spin around the frozen lake. ⏲ *45 min. 5 Yiheyuan Lu. Free admission; admission may be regulated during politically sensitive times such as June 4, the anniversary of the Tian'anmen massacre. Enter the university from its east gate. Metro: Wudaokou (Beida's east gate is about 3.2km/2 miles west of the metro stop). From metro stop, take taxi.*

❷ ★ kids Old Summer Palace (Yuanming Yuan). Comprised of three separate imperial gardens, the ruins at Yuanming Yuan are hauntingly beautiful. Although this is a more recent construction than the New Summer Palace (see bullet ❹ below), it is often referred to as the Old Summer Palace because it was not rebuilt after the French and British troops burned it down during the Second Opium War of 1856–60. A few restorations have begun, including **Wanhua Zhen (10,000 Flowers Maze),** a nicely reconstructed labyrinth in the Changchun Yuan (Garden of Eternal Spring). Park management and the district government recently came under environmental fire when they decided to line the park's lakes with impermeable plastic tarp (thereby destroying natural habitats and creating an underwater world of anaerobic sludge) to save on water bills and raise water levels for a duck-boat business. The lakes have since been restored but are drained in the winter. During the warmer seasons, stake out a spot on one of the pavilions overlooking the lake and take in the gorgeous view of colorful lotuses and their giant leaves floating on the water's surface. ⏲ *1½ hr.; head over just before lunch to avoid crowds. Qinghua Xilù 28.* ☎ *010/6262-8501. Admission ¥10;*

Peking University.

Ruins of the Old Summer Palace.

¥25 to enter Xi Yang Lou. Nov–Mar 7:30am–5:30pm, Apr 7am–6:30pm; May–Aug 7am–7pm; Sept–Oct 7am–6:30pm.

⑤ ★ Aman Resort. It's a bit of a splurge, but given the slim pickings in northwestern Beijing, this is an ideal place for a relaxed afternoon tea served next to a koi pond in the city's most luxurious resort. *1 Gongmenqian Lu, eastern side of the Summer Palace.* ☎ *010/5987-9999.* *$$$.*

④ ★ New Summer Palace (Yihe Yuan). This palace park covers roughly 290 hectares (717 acres) and is bordered by Kunming Lake in the south and Longevity Hill (Wanshou Shan) in the north. The collection of halls, pavilions, and temples beside Kunming Lake was a favorite haunt of dowager empress Cixi (1835–1908), who preferred it to the Forbidden City. The **Hall of Happiness and Longevity** was Cixi's former residence, first built in 1750 and rebuilt in 1887. Walk west and you will enter the aptly named **Long Corridor,** which zigzags for 728m (2,388 ft.), culminating in the Boat of Purity and Ease. The "boat" is a hull-shaped structure carved out of rock. It acts as a base for a two-story marble superstructure that now houses cafes serving instant coffee and snacks. On the way to the boat, you'll pass the **Tower of Buddhist Fragrance,** nestled atop Longevity Hill. The steep climb to the top is rewarded with a great view over sweeping yellow roofs and the lake's Seventeen-Arch Bridge. ⏱ *2 hr. 19 Xinjiangongmen Lu.* ☎ *010/6288-1144. Admission ¥30 for the grounds, ¥60 for the all-inclusive lian piao Apr–Oct; ¥20 and ¥50, respectively Nov–Mar.*

⑤ Fragrant Hills (Xiang Shan Gongyuan). This outdoor playground has been around since 1168, covering 160 hectares (395 acres). The highest peak resembles an incense burner. Take the chairlift to the top for a leisurely look over Beijing's northwest district, ¥30 one-way, ¥50 round-trip. The multitude of pools, pavilions, temples, villas, and ancient trees make it an idyllic picnic spot far removed from the din of the city traffic. In 1949, Mao Zedong stayed here while commanding the Yangtze Crossing campaign, which clinched victory over the Nationalist forces. The building that played witness to this shining moment in Communist history is

The New Summer Palace.

Seventeen-Arch Bridge and Kunming Lake.

now maintained as a shrine. ⏲ *1 hr. Beijing Xibeijiao Xishan Donglu.* ☎ *010/6259-1155. Admission ¥10 Apr–Nov; ¥5 Dec–Mar.*

6 **kids** **Da Zhong Si**. This Qing dynasty (1644–1911/12) temple now houses the Ancient Bell Museum (Gu Zhong Bowuguan). It was once

known as Juesheng Si (Awakened Life Temple), but clearly there wasn't enough awakening going on, so a 47-ton bell was transported here on ice sleds in 1743. The third hall on the right houses clangers garnered from around Beijing. Some were donated by eunuchs wishing the relevant emperor long life, with

Chinese 101

The place to hone your Chinese language skills is the Wudaokou area, with its bars, Wi-Fi cafes, international grocery shops, and language schools catering to the foreign students who live nearby. Besides Beida (see "Peking University," above), Tsinghua University and the Beijing Language and Culture University are also nearby. All three universities attract hordes of international students who typically spend a semester or two abroad to study Chinese. But if you don't have 4 months to devote to Mandarin study, you are better off at one of the many private language schools on Chengfu Lu that offer drop-in classes. I recommend **Diqiucun (Global Village;** 35 Chengfu Lu, northwest of the metro stop; ☎ 010/6253-7737). They have 1- and 2-hour listening, speaking, and reading classes that run daily, plus plenty of beginner classes. Classes are cheap: just ¥30 per class, ¥32 to ¥64 for the textbook. If you're lucky, you'll catch one that is just starting. Otherwise, you'll have to brave a beginner's class that is one or more chapters into the book. They also offer intermediate and advanced classes (colloquial Chinese for business meetings, anyone?).

New Year's Eve. Visitors rub the handles of the Qianlong emperor's old washbasin, and climb up narrow steps to make a wish while throwing coins through a hole in the top of the bell. But it is no longer the "King of Bells"—that honor now goes to the 50-ton bell housed in the Altar to the Century (Zhonghua Shiji Tan), constructed in 1999 to prove that China, too, could waste money on the millennium. ⏱ *25 min.* ☎ *010/ 6255-0819. Admission ¥10; 9am–4pm. ¥2 to climb the Bell Tower. 31A Bei San Huan Xi Lu. Metro: Da Zhong Si.*

7️⃣ **Sculpting in Time.** Head to Wudaokou, a coffee shop/bar/ bookstore area that has sprung up around the metro stop of the same name. It is a hub of activity, where foreign students come to hang out, study, and party. Sculpting in Time is in the heart of all this young enthusi-asm and serves some excellent cof-fee with free wireless Internet to boot. *Bldg. 12 Huaqing Jiayuan 1 Chengfu Lu, just west of Wudaokou metro stop.* ☎ *010/8286-7026. $.* ●

The chalkboard menu at Sculpting in Time.

hundreds of donors' names scrawled on their sides. The main attraction is housed in the rear hall, carved inside and out with 230,000 Chinese and Sanskrit characters. The big bell tolls once a year, on

Fragrant Hills Park.

Beijing for Contemporary Art Lovers

Map Area

BEIJING

- Summer Palace
- Chaoyang Park
- Forbidden City
- Tian'anmen Square
- Temple of Heaven

706 North First Street

798 East Street

Jiuxianqiao North Road 酒仙桥北路

706 Road

797 Road

798 Road

798 Main Second Street

798 Main First Street

798 West Street

707 Street

797 Main Street

718 Street

Sevenstar Road

798 Dashanzi Yishu Qu Zhongxin

Sevenstar West Street

500 ft

100 m

Jiuxianqiao Road 酒仙桥路

① **Timezone 8 Bookstore**
现代书店艺术书屋

② **The Hub of the 798 Dashanzi Art District**
798 大山子艺术区中心

②A **798 Photo Gallery**
百年印象摄影画廊

②B **798 Space**
时态空间

②C **Beijing-Tokyo Art Projects**
东京画廊

②D **Ullens Center for Contemporary Art**
尤伦斯当代艺术中心

③ **Beijing Commune**
北京公社

④ **Long March Space**
长征空间

⑤ **Yin Shu + EA West**
银殊艺饰店

⑥ **Faurschou Gallery**
林冠画廊

⑦ **Café Pause**
闲着也是闲着咖啡店

Previous page: Sun Yat-sen suit in 798 Art Center.

Beijing is China's most vibrant artistic hub, *the* place where avant-garde artists and curators rub shoulders with international art dealers and critics. The epicenter of China's contemporary art world is the 798 Dashanzi Art District. Since 2001, artists have converted this cluster of abandoned Bauhaus-style factories into the country's top studios and galleries. We'll show you not only Beijing's best contemporary artworks, but also the best spaces for viewing them. Avoid the area on Mondays, when many of the galleries are closed. START: **Taxi to 4 Jiuxianqiao Lu.**

Travel Tip

Taxis aren't allowed into the complex, so you'll have to walk 3 long blocks on the number four main road until you see the sign for **Timezone 8**, an art bookstore on your left.

❶ Timezone 8 Bookstore.

Here you'll find the most up-to-date information on the district's art gallery openings and closings, and the area's most current maps. It's worth beginning your tour here since things change very quickly at Danshanzi. 🕐 *10 min. 4 Jiuxianqiao Lu, D03-3-1.* ☎ *010/8456-0336. www. timezone8.com. Daily 10am–8pm.*

❷ ★★ The Hub of the 798 Dashanzi Art District.** While the area of art galleries has grown

Gallery 798 Space.

considerably in the last few years, this is where local artists set up the area's first studios and galleries in 2001. From the main road, turn

Timezone 8 Bookstore.

right, and down the corridor on your right, you'll see the **2A** **798 Photo Gallery.** ☎ 010/6438-1784. 4 Jiuxianqiao Lu, Taoci 3 Alley. www.798photogallery.cn. Daily 10am–6pm. On your left is the Bauhaus-style, high-ceilinged **2B** **798 Space,** formerly used as a military factory, now hosting art and multimedia installations and performances. ☎ 010/6437-6248. 4 Jiuxianqiao Lu, Taoci 3 Alley. www.798space.com. Tues–Sun 11am–6pm. Farther down the hallway on your right is the **2C** **Beijing-Tokyo Art Projects,** which often hosts avant-garde installations. 🕐 30 min. ☎ 010/8457-3245. 4 Jiuxianqiao Lu, E02-0-10. www.Tokyogallery.com. Tues–Sun 10:30am–6:30pm (to 5:30pm Nov–Mar). The **2D** **Ullens Center for Contemporary Art,** Beijing's premier art

A ring display at Yin Shu + EA West.

museum, was set up by a pair of art collectors from Europe. It features the city's most avant-garde exhibitions. 🕐 1 hr. ☎ 010/8459-9269. 4 Jiuxianqiao Lu. www.ucca.org.cn. Tues–Sun 10am–7pm.

3 **Beijing Commune Gallery.** This recently opened gallery represents established Chinese contemporary artists but also takes chances and displays young emerging Chinese artists. 🕐 15 min. ☎ 010/8456-2862. 4 Jiuxianqiao Lu. www.beijingcommune.com. Daily 10am–6pm.

4 **Long March Space.** You will find provoking, and often interactive, installations at this gigantic warehouse space. 🕐 15 min. ☎ 010/5978-9768. 4 Jiuxianqiao Lu, D01-0-1. www.longmarchspace.com. Tues–Sun 11am–7pm.

Ullens Center of Contemporary Art.

Faurschou Gallery.

5 ★ Yin Shu +EA West. Local artist Man Kaihui creates gutsy earrings and necklaces. We love her unique, industrial-looking jewelry, which stands out in a country known for more feminine styles. This boutique also contains locally designed sweaters and dresses with a softer touch. ⏲ *15 min.* ☎ *010/6437-3432. 4 Jiuxianqiao Lu, Tues–Sun 10am–6pm.*

6 Faurschou Gallery. Headquartered in Copenhagen, this large, airy gallery displays a mix of international and Chinese contemporary art. ⏲ *15 min.* ☎ *010/5978-9316. 2 Jiuxianqiao Lu. www.faurschou.com. Tues–Sun 10am–6pm.*

7 ★ Café Pause. This delightfully cozy cafe is owned by two European expats and serves lattes in cups the size of your head. We also love the fusion-style munchies, such as the spinach and cheese dumplings. *2 Jiuxianqiao Lu.* ☎ *010/6431-6214. $.*

"Hello, I'm an Art Student"

Be leery of any English-speaking youngsters who claim to be art students and offer to take you to a special exhibit of their work. This is a scam. The art, which you will be compelled to buy, almost always consists of assembly-line reproductions of famous (or not so famous) paintings offered at prices several dozen times higher than their actual value.

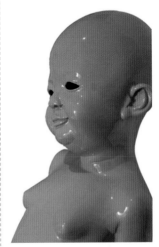

The art is often intriguing at Long March Space.

Red **Beijing**

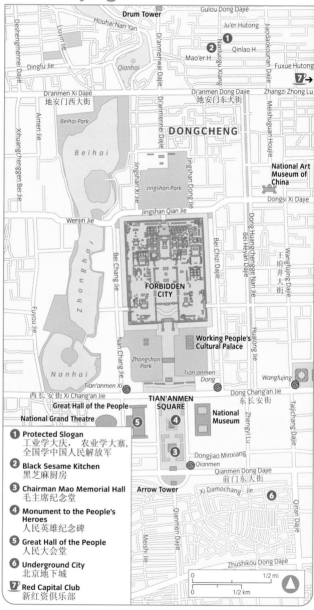

1 **Protected Slogan**
工业学大庆，农业学大寨，
全国学中国人民解放军

2 **Black Sesame Kitchen**
黑芝麻厨房

3 **Chairman Mao Memorial Hall**
毛主席纪念堂

4 **Monument to the People's Heroes**
人民英雄纪念碑

5 **Great Hall of the People**
人民大会堂

6 **Underground City**
北京地下城

7 **Red Capital Club**
新红资俱乐部

0   1/2 mi

0   1/2 km

Despite the brutal excesses of the Cultural Revolution, Mao retains a heroic status in Beijing, as evidenced by his beaming portrait smack in the middle of Tian'anmen Square. His ultimate legacy in modern Beijing remains undecided; the official position today is that he was 70% right and 30% wrong. This tour will take you to glossy symbols of Communist China, as well as to hidden relics that while less glamorous, are evocative, chilly reminders of China's recent past. START: **Nanluoguxiang, north entrance.**

1 Protected Slogan. Nanluoguxiang is a historical *hutong*, or alley, that underwent a massive face-lift a few years ago. During renovations, an original Cultural Revolution slogan painted on a building's brick face was uncovered. While the rest of the alley was treated to a fresh coat of somber gray paint, the resident community group decided that the slogan should be preserved. The red-painted characters state: "Learn industry from Daqing, agriculture from the model villages, and the whole nation should learn from the People's Liberation Army!" ⏱ *15 min. East side of Nanluoguxiang, across from the Plastered T-shirt shop at 61 Nanluoguxiang.*

2 Black Sesame Kitchen. You'll have to book ahead, but this cooking school and restaurant (owned by the author of this very guide) will teach you how to make Chairman Mao's favorite dish, hongshao rou, by request. *Next To Wiggly Jiggly Pub. At 3 Heizhima Hutong (call for exact directions).* ☎ *0136/9147-4408. Cooking classes every Thurs 11am–1:30pm and Sat 1–4pm. Dinners every Fri 7–10pm. Reservations required. Private bookings also accepted.*

3 Chairman Mao Memorial Hall (Mao Zhuxi Jinnian Guan). The bright lighting, Mao's somber state, and the Chinese tourists pushing you from behind combine for an unsettling experience. You'll be rushed through the room at a brisk pace, but not so brisk that Mao's tint and suspiciously waxy pallor go unnoticed.

Keeping Up Appearances

The decision to preserve Mao's body was made hours after his death in 1976 and went against his wishes to be cremated. China didn't have the technical know-how, and due to frosty relations, experts couldn't ask the USSR for help. So they turned to neighboring Vietnam, where doctors had already embalmed Ho Chi Minh. However, Mao was pumped so full of formaldehyde that his face and body swelled beyond recognition. Doctors drained the corpse and got it back to an acceptable shape, but in a moment of Madame Tussaud inspiration (indeed, two researchers were even sent to the famous waxworks museum in London to gather information), they created a wax model of the Great Helmsmen just in case. Rumor has it that the body is decaying rapidly and that the wax model is usually on display during the mausoleum's short open hours.

Family-Friendly Beijing

The Chinese love children and Beijing is generally a kid-friendly place. If your children are falling asleep on the Great Wall and dragging their feet at the temples, head to these places for some good old family fun.

Bring your kids to play at **Ritan Park** (Ritan Bei Lu; (☎ 010/8561-6301), open daily 6am to 8pm. Plenty of mini-Beijingers are here on the weekend tumbling around on the trampolines or in the inflatable playhouse. Your kids may want to join a game of "jianzi," or Chinese hacky sack.

Beijing's answer to Disneyland is ★ **Happy Valley (Huan Le Gu;** Xiao Wu Ji Bei Lu, Dong Si Huan [East Fourth Ring Road]; ☎ 010/6738-3333; http://bj.happyvalley.com.cn/park). This theme park features stomach-turning roller coasters, Shangri-La Land, a Mayan Aztec village, and a Greek town. Lines for rides can be 3 hours long, so arrive early and avoid the weekends. Open daily November to March 9:30am to 6pm and April to November 9:30am to 10pm. Admission is ¥160 adults, ¥80 kids 1.2 to 1.4m (4 ft.–4 ft. 6 in.), free for kids under 1.2m (4 ft.).

Arouse your child's inner techie at **Sony ExploraScience,** inside Chaoyang Park (Chaoyang Gongyuan; ☎ 010/6501-8800). This museum has live science shows (in Chinese) and plenty of interactive exhibits. We love the swipe cards, which act as keys that unlock the secrets of each science station (English text provided). Open Monday to Friday from 9:30am to 5:30pm and Saturday to Sunday until 6:30pm. Admission is ¥30 adults, ¥20 students, and free for kids under 1.2m (4 ft.). Buy your tickets at the park's south or east gates and you won't have to buy park entry tickets.

If you're braving Beijing's winter season, head to **Houhai Lake** for some **outdoor skating.** Admission is free to skate on certain parts of the lake, such as near Yinding Qiao (Silver Ingot Bridge). The walled-off area near Lotus Lane maintains the ice surface (with a shovel, not a Zamboni), plays music, and charges ¥20. Skate rentals vary according to vendors. Usually open November to February.

❹ Monument to the People's Heroes (Renmin Yixiong Jinianbe). Walk to the north side of Mao's Mausoleum to view the first thing the Communists ordered built when they took command of Beijing in 1949. The monument consists of eight relief panels featuring China's historical heroes. The north side (facing Mao's portrait) features characters in Mao's calligraphy, proclaiming the eternal fame of the people's heroes. The south side contains words by Zhou Enlai, a powerful leader of the Chinese Communist Party, who served as premier of the Peoples' Republic of China from 1949 to 1976. ⏱ *5 min.* *South end of Tian'anmen Square.* *Free admission.*

5 Great Hall of the People.
Walk to the northwest corner of
Tian'anmen Square to see this quint-
essential Communist-style building
up close. If your visit doesn't coin-
cide with pressing political matters
or a national holiday, the tour will
take you through a vast interior,
marked by typical Communist-style
largesse. ⏱ *25 min. Northwest corner of Tian'anmen Square, ticket
booth at south end of the building.
Open daily 8:15am–3pm, but subject
to changes for special events, so call
ahead. Bags and cameras are not
allowed in the hall.* ☎ *010/8308-
4776. Admission ¥30 adults; ¥15
students.*

**6 ★ Underground City (Dixia
Cheng).** A 5-minute train ride will
take you to my favorite stop on this
tour. This underground labyrinth
lacks the impressive, affected gran-
deur of Tian'anmen Square, but has
its own, "authentic" Communist feel
to it: damp, in disrepair, and decorated with swaths of material pat-
terned in army-fatigue green. The
walls are adorned with original Cultural Revolution posters, several of

Decor at the Red Capital Club.

which instruct citizens on what to
do in the event of a biological or
nuclear attack. ("If you see the fire-
ball from an atom bomb explosion,
quickly proceed to a street corner
and lie face down on the ground.")
There is a good silk market at the
end of the first part of the tour—
make sure the guide continues
behind the market, which he or she
may not immediately do because
the tunnels are wet and not well
ventilated. ⏱ *30 min. 62 Xi Damochang Jie, Chongwen Qu (from metro
stop, walk west; take the 1st left
onto Qinian Da Jie, then take the 2nd
right. The entrance is on the south
side, approx. 800m [2,625 ft.] in).*
☎ *010/6702-2657. Admission ¥20.
Daily 8:30am–5:30pm. Metro: Chongwen Men, exit D.*

7 Red Capital Club. Take a
5-minute taxi ride north to experience one man's effort to cash in on
Communist sentiment: American
owner Laurence Brahm has dedi-
cated his bar/restaurant to China's
red capitalists. (Red capitalists are
entrepreneurs who amassed for-
tunes by doing business in the gray
zone between Communism and
capitalism during China's period of
opening and reform in the late '70s
and '80s.) The Red Capital Club is
decked out in authentic antique furniture and decorations, including a
vintage Red Flag limo once used by
China's top Communist leaders. The
club attracts a mix of tourists and
well-to-do expats and Chinese
patrons. Order yourself a Mao-tai
and ask to take a peek at their wine
cellar, a converted bomb shelter
that was originally part of the
Underground City. *66 Dongsi Jiutiao.*
☎ *010/8401-6152. $$.*

Beijing **by Bicycle**

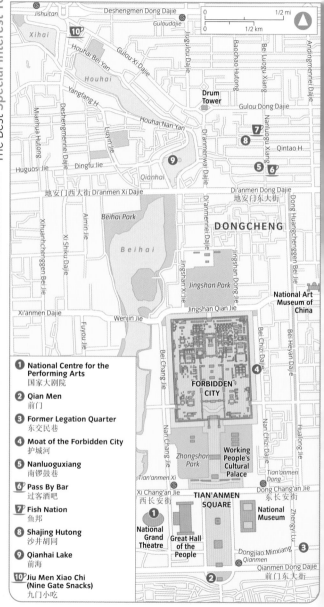

1. **National Centre for the Performing Arts**
   国家大剧院

2. **Qian Men**
   前门

3. **Former Legation Quarter**
   东交民巷

4. **Moat of the Forbidden City**
   护城河

5. **Nanluoguxiang**
   南锣鼓巷

6. **Pass By Bar**
   过客酒吧

7. **Fish Nation**
   鱼邦

8. **Shajing Hutong**
   沙井胡同

9. **Qianhai Lake**
   前海

10. **Jiu Men Xiao Chi (Nine Gate Snacks)**
    九门小吃

Though cars are quickly clogging up the roads, Beijingers still cycle to work, to shopping malls, and even to bars for a night out on the town. Bicycles in China carry the same loads as trucks—we've seen cyclists pulling wagons carrying everything from refrigerators and computers to a dozen rusty bicycles! But for your own cycling tour of Beijing, you won't need to haul anything except this guidebook and a bottle of water. The entire tour should take approximately 3 hours at a leisurely pace. START: **East gate of Jingshan Park.**

Biking Tips

Grab a bicycle from Cycle China, 12 Jingshan Dong Lu (☎ **010/6402-5653;** www.cyclechina.com). They rent Giant city and mountain bikes in excellent condition, and they carry frames for taller people. Make sure to pass on the left and give way to cyclers in front of you.

Bike south from Jingshan Dong Lu, turn right at the T-intersection onto Jingshan Qian Jie, and follow the road as it curves south (left) around the Forbidden City. You are now on Beichang Jie. Go straight until you come to the western corner of Tian'anmen Gate. Cross Dong Chang'an Jie.

1 National Centre for the Performing Arts. Dreamed up by French architect Paul Andreu, this space age–looking building was completed in 2008. The giant, dome-shaped structure has been nicknamed "Jidanke'r" (The Egg Shell) by Beijingers. The project has had its share of controversy; many think it's a big waste of money and that the futuristic design clashes with the surrounding buildings. Final plans call for the entire structure to float like an island in the middle of a lake. At night, the theater's semi-transparent facade will allow passersby to peek in at performances in one of the three auditoriums, a feature meant to highlight the building's public nature. *West of the Great Hall of the People, Tian'anmen Square.* ☎ *010/6655-0871.*

Continue south along Tian'anmen W. Road, past the Great Hall of the People and Mao's Mausoleum.

The futuristic National Grand Theater.

2 Qian Men. Qian Men is actually two separate towers. They once formed the main entrance to Beijing, which was walled off before Mao's reign. The one north of the main street (Qian Men Dong Dajie) is Jian Lou, or Arrow Tower. To the south is Zhengyang Men, a towering remnant of the city wall through which emperors passed on their annual procession from the Forbidden City to the Temple of Heaven. At the top of Zhengyang Men, an enjoyable photo exhibition depicts Beijing's 1949 markets, temples, and hutongs. Make sure to park your bike somewhere safe, preferably a place that has an attendant (the KFC on the southwest corner is a good spot). *South side of Tian'anmen Square.* ☎ *010/6522-9382. Admission ¥20 summer; ¥10 winter.*

Turn left onto Tian'anmen Square E. Road, biking back along the eastern side of the square. Turn right onto Xin Da Li (at the pedestrian walkway just north of Mao's Mausoleum), and head up the small hill. Turn right at the T-intersection and bike until you come to a second T-intersection at Dongxiao Minxiang.

The Forbidden City's moat.

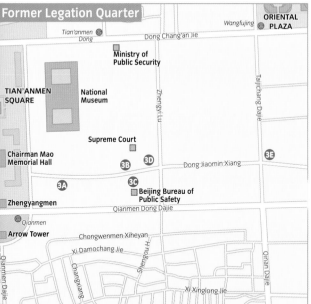

Former Legation Quarter

Tian'anmen Dong

Dong Chang'an Jie

Wangfujing

ORIENTAL PLAZA

Ministry of Public Security

TIAN'ANMEN SQUARE

National Museum

Zhengyi Lu

Taijichang Dajie

Supreme Court

Chairman Mao Memorial Hall

3B **3D**

3E

Dong Jiaomin Xiang

3A

3C

Beijing Bureau of Public Safety

Zhengyangmen

Qianmen Dong Dajie

Qianmen

Arrow Tower

Chongwenmen Xiheyan

Xi Damochang Jie

Shengyu H.

Qinan Dajie

Qianmen Dajie

Changxiang

Xi Xinglong Jie

---

3 ★ **Former Legation Quarter (Shiguan Jie).** This is where the embassies of the major powers of the day, international banks, a post office, and other outposts of Western civilization were located between 1861 and 1959. When allied forces occupied Beijing, they set up their headquarters here, and it was off-limits to the Chinese. At the time, an imperial temple was within the cordoned-off area, which meant that the emperor had to go through formal diplomatic entry-exit procedures in order to worship the ancestors—a huge humiliation for the Chinese. In front of you at 44 Dongjiao Minxiang is the building that once housed **3A** **the former American Embassy.** Keep riding

east (left) on Dongjiao Minxiang. On your left you'll see number 27, where the **3B** **Russian Embassy** once stood—it is now the back entrance to China's Supreme Court. The red brick building across the road is **3C** **the former Hong Kong Shanghai Bank of China (HSBC).** Farther up is 15 Dongjiao Minxiang, currently home to China's State Council. Note the slate blue and flowery white decorations above the door, a nod to the building's past occupant, **3D** **the old French Embassy.** Keep biking east, across Zhengyi Lu. On the northeast corner, after you cross Taijichang Dajie, is the **3E** **Dongjiao Minxiang Catholic Church,** the only building from legation times that is still in service.

From the church, head north on Taijichang Dajie until you hit Dongchang'an Jie. Turn left and ride until you get to Nan Chizi

Dajie (east side of the Forbidden City, marked by a big red entranceway). Head north until you get to the Dong Hua Men intersection. Turn left, past the parked cars, and turn left again to ride along:

4 The Moat of the Forbidden City.

The moat that surrounds the Forbidden City is 3.7km (2⅓ miles) long—the length of 35 football fields! Soil that was dug out to make the moat was used to build the central hill in Jingshan Park. As you follow the road (Dong Hua Men Dajie), you'll cut straight through the entrance to the Forbidden City, zipping past Taihe Men (the Gate of Great Harmony), and come out on the other side. Follow the road as it curves around the moat.

You should be at the intersection of Xi Hua Men and Nanchang Jie. Head in a northeast direction until you get to Bei He Yan Dajie, then ride straight north. Take a left at Di'an Men Dong Dajie and then your first right (at the pedestrian walkway).

5 Nanluoguxiang.

In 2006, this crooked road was smoothed out with bricks, and the smaller shops and restaurants were ordered to clean up their entrances and hang up bilingual signs. Nanluoguxiang is home to a mix of locals who have lived in the area for generations and foreigners—including us—who want to feel as though they're living in Old Beijing. We love the neighborly atmosphere and feel lucky to be experiencing a way of life that is quickly dying out.

There are plenty of bars, cafes, and restaurants on Nanluoguxiang. **6 Pass By Bar** (108 Nanluoguxiang; ☎ 010/8403-8004; $) was the one that started it all, and the tastefully redone courtyard complex here has a great, relaxing ambience. But if you want drinkable coffee, head to the cozy rooftop of **7 Fish Nation** (31 Nanluoguxiang; ☎ 010/6401-3249; $), where we often go for our caffeine or french fry fix.

If you're at Pass By Bar head north, south if you're at Fish Nation. Turn west onto Shajing Hutong.

8 Shajing Hutong.

This alley has two courtyard houses with exteriors in perfect condition. Number 8 is used by the armed forces and boasts a three-car garage.

Turn left at the end of the road and follow the road as it curves around. Turn left onto Fangzhuanchang hutong (there's a grocery on the corner). Follow the alley to the main road, Di'anmenwai Dajie, where you'll turn left, then take your first right at the bank (ICBC). You're now at the northern corner of Qianhai.

Sign marking Nanluoguxiang Road.

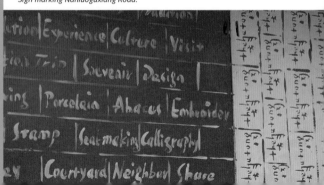

The courtyard at Pass by Bar.

⑨ Qianhai Lake. Bike north and, once you pass the congestion around the bridge, this turns into a fabulous bike ride along the lakes. Stop in at any of the sites, as you wish (see "Back Lake Ramble," p 38); other-wise pedal along at a leisurely pace.

Stay on the eastern side of the lake (Qianhai Beiyan/Houhai Bei-yan). Bike past the former residence of Song Qingling, and in about 300m (984 ft.), you'll see a decorative wooden gate lakeside, and a corresponding smaller sign with photos of various dishes on the right. They point to:

⑩ ★ Jiu Men Xiao Chi (Nine Gate Snacks). These stalls moved here from the city's historical Qian-men area in early 2006. When you enter, head left to buy a food card (any money you don't use will be refunded when you return the card). The main aisle is full of Mus-lim stalls, while the ones in the doorway serve pork. You cannot take non-Muslim food into the main aisle, so if you want to pick up a plate of deep-fried pork and onion rolls at one of the entrance stalls, do it after you order some tasty, halal-friendly dishes. Tables are dot-ted throughout the restaurant, and

inside is a stage with traditional Chinese music performances. 1 Xiaoyou Hutong. $.

Head back to Houhai Beiyan, fol-low the road around the lake, and cross Yinding Qiao (Silver Ingot Bridge). Continue south around the lake, along Qianhai Nanyan, until you can exit onto the main street (Di'anmen Xidajie). From here, follow the main roads back to Cycle China to return the bikes.

The food stalls known as Nine Gates.

Beijing: Past, Present & Future

Dong Sanhuan Bei Lu

Dong Sanhuan Zhong Lu

Panjiayuan Lu

Ritan Park

Jianguomenwai Dajie

Jingsong Lu

1

Chaoyangmen Nan Dajie

Guangqumennei Dajie

Beijing Amusement Park

Zuo'anmen D.B. Lu

Nansanhuan Dong Lu

Dongsi Nan Dajie

Wangfujing Dajie

Qinan Dajie

Tiantan Lu

Temple of Heaven Park

2

FORBIDDEN CITY

Dong Chang'an Jie

TIAN'ANMEN SQUARE

Qianmen Dajie

3

Behai

Zhonghai

Nanhai

Xi Chang'an Jie

You'anmen Dong Binhe Lu

Wangfangting Park

Xidan Bei Dajie

Taoranting Park

Nan Sanhuan Xi Lu

Fuxingmen Bei Dajie

Guang'anmennei Dajie

Fucheng Lu

Guang'anmen Bei Binhe Lu

Yuyuantan Park

Yuyuantan

Tize Lu

Fuxingmenwai Dajie

Lianhuachi Dong Lu

4

Xi Sanhuan Nan Lu

1 mi

1 km

1 Panjiayuan
潘家园

2 Beijing Municipal
Planning Exhibition Hall
北京规划展览馆

3 Lao She Teahouse
老舍茶楼

4 Capital Museum
首都博物馆

In several short decades, Mao suits have given way to blue jeans, traditional brick courtyards have morphed into skyscrapers, and millions of bicycle owners have upgraded to cars. This tour is meant to give you a glimpse of Beijing's past, present, and future—all of which exist side by side in this rapidly transitioning capital.

START: **Panjiayuan Lu.**

❶ ★★★ **Panjiayuan.** Mao memorabilia, black-and-white photographs of Beijing's dusty streets, and traditional minority costumes can be found in the bustling stalls of Beijing's best antiques and curio market. We prefer coming on weekends for the wonderful buzz. Vendors from all over China convene here: Folk artists, Tibetans in dark canvas robes, and hill tribespeople from rural parts of China wearing brightly embroidered dresses begin pulling cartloads of traditional wares to the market starting just after sunrise, though the market's gates don't open until 8am. The weekdays are less busy, but sometimes better for bargaining since there are fewer tourists. No one can vouch for the authenticity of the supposed

antiques that are offered here, so bargain hard. See "Bare-Bones Bargaining," p 64. ⏱ *2 hr.; go early and on the weekend, if possible. Panjiayuan Lu. No phone. Free admission. Daily 8am–4pm.*

❷ ★ kids **Beijing Municipal Planning Exhibition Hall.** The 20-minute taxi ride from Panjiayuan (if the traffic is decent) will feel like a huge leap forward in time once you're immersed in this high-tech museum, which gives you of a glimpse of tomorrow's Beijing. Several of the exhibitions are interactive, including the scale model of Beijing that you can actually walk on. We highly recommend the short movies, offered at half-hour intervals and in English on request. The 3-D movie,

Goods for sale at Panjiayuan.

complete with the funny glasses, tells the history of Beijing's development. The 4-D movie—more like a ride at an amusement park—takes you on a tour of Beijing's future subway lines, which will supposedly connect any two points in Beijing in less than an hour. Even if it is propaganda, it's still good fun. ⏱ *90 min. 20 Qianmen Dong Lu.* ☎ *010/6702-4559. www.bjghzl.com.cn. Admission ¥30; ¥10 additional for each movie. Tues–Sun 9am–5pm (4pm last entry). Subway: Qianmen.*

③ ★ Lao She Teahouse. A 15-minute walk from the Exhibition Hall, this old teahouse recently underwent a slick makeover, but still offers the same traditional tea and afternoon musical performances with Chinese instruments like the zither and the erhu, a Chinese violin. *Bldg. 3, Zhengyang shichang Qianmen Xi Dajie.* ☎ *010/6303-6830. $.*

④ ★★ Capital Museum. A 30-minute subway ride (take a taxi, if you're feeling lazy) will take you to one of China's best-curated and -designed museums. The Capital Museum displays artifacts from Beijing's past and present, including bronzes, photographs, and models of traditional courtyard gates. The fifth floor has interesting exhibitions on Beijing folk customs and the Peking Opera, with live performances on Saturday from 10am to noon. It's a good way to sample Peking Opera music (which isn't to everyone's liking) since you can always move on to the next exhibition without the embarrassment of sneaking out of a theater. The basement cafe offers an impressive range of international foods. ⏱ *90 min. 16 Fuxingmenwai Dajie.* ☎ *010/6337-0491. www.capitalmuseum.org.cn. Free admission with passport. Tues–Sun 9am–5pm (4pm last entry). Subway: Muxidi.* ●

Checking out the scale model of Beijing.

Back Lake **Ramble**

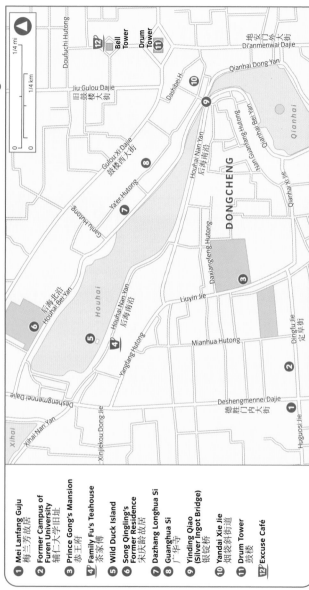

Previous page: A shop selling musical instruments in Liulichang.

The circuit around and near Houhai (Mandarin for Back Lake) is far and away the best walk in Beijing. Historic imperial residences rub shoulders with new yuppie cafes, while crumbling residences abut renovated multimillion dollar lake-view residences. This walk can be done at any time of the day, though if you start in the midafternoon, you'll be rewarded by romantic sunset views at your walk's end. START: **Mei Lanfang Guju. Corner of Deshengmen Nei Dajie and Dingfu Jie.**

① Mei Lanfang Guju. Look for the red lanterns outside this superbly preserved courtyard residence. This home once belonged to Peking Opera star Mei Lanfang, who rose to the height of his fame in 1935. The pictures of the singer displayed within demonstrate the wide range of expressions used in this art form. 🕐 *15 min. 9 Huguosi Dajie.* ☎ *010/6618-3598. Admission ¥10. 9am–4pm (Tues–Sun).*

Furen University.

② Former Campus of Furen University. The original campus of Furen University, a Catholic institution set up by Chinese priests, was built in 1925. Shuttered after the Communists came to power, the institution moved to Taiwan. Note the ornate facade featuring an arched doorway and the traditional sloping Chinese roof. *1 Dingfu Jie.*

③ Prince Gong's Mansion. This is the most lavish courtyard residence in the Back Lakes. The 1777 mansion was occupied by Heshen, a corrupt official who was rumored to be the emperor Qianlong's lover. Later, it became the home of Prince Gong, who negotiated on behalf of China at the end of the Second Opium War. 🕐 *30 min.*

Prince Gong's Mansion has many rockeries and pavilions to explore.

Relax with a cup of tea at Family Fu's Teahouse.

14A Liuyin Jie. ☎ *010/6616-8149.
Admission ¥20; ¥60 for a guided
tour with an opera performance.
8:30am–4:30pm.*

④ **Family Fu's Teahouse.** At this
lakeside teahouse you can relax on
Ming dynasty furniture while sipping
longjing, a green tea from Hang-
zhou, one of China's famed tea-pro-
ducing areas. The English- speaking
owner is particularly friendly. *Hou-
hai Park.* ☎ *010/6616-0725. $$.*

⑤ **Wild Duck Island.** Beijing is
full of loopy attractions, including
this man-made island built of steel

Worshipping at Guanghua Si.

for the area's ducks. March is mat-
ing season on the island and a par-
ticularly busy time. *Houhai Lake.*

⑥ **Song Qingling's Former
Residence.** This former imperial
palace once famously housed the
wife of Sun Yat-sen, modern China's
founder. This feminist hero later
became a friend of Mao's and a
Communist sympathizer. ⏱ *30 min.
46 Houhai Bei Yan.* ☎ *010/6404-
4205. Admission ¥20. 9am–5pm (to
4:30pm in winter).*

⑦ **Dazhang Longhua Si.** As you
continue along the lake you'll pass
the outdoor exercise equipment
(which senior citizens will probably
be using). Keep an eye out for the
gate of this 1719 temple. Though
it's now the grounds of a kindergar-
ten, the facade, with intricate animal
shaped stone gargoyles, has been
nicely preserved. ⏱ *5 min. 23 Hou-
hai Bei Yan.*

⑧ **Guanghua Si.** A Buddhist
temple dating from the Yuán
dynasty (1279–1368), this complex
originally comprised more than 20
buildings; only a few of the buildings
remain. In residence are at least 20
monks, many from southern China.
Admission is allowed on the 1st and
15th days of the lunar month, when
the temple is filled with locals pray-
ing for the success of their latest

business ventures. Though it's not officially open to the public at other times, monks have snuck us in more than once. China's last known eunuch, Sun Yaotinga, was the caretaker for 2 decades, before dying here in 1996. ⏱ *10 min. 31 Ya'er Hutong, Gulou Xi Dajie. No phone.*

⑨ Yinding Qiao (Silver Ingot Bridge). This bridge separates Houhai from Qianhai (Front Lake). It's usually a mess of tourists, aggressive rickshaws, and cars. ⏱ *5 min.*

⑩ Yandai Xie Jie. Walk away from the bridge and turn right at the sign that reads MASTER OF FOLK ARTS AND CRAFTS FINE WORK SALE. This touristy pedestrian street houses a few gems. Number 63 on the left, a folk-art store, features stylish Chinese pillow covers, framed paper cuts, and cloth coasters. Number 20 on the right sells cute totes and lipstick cases with Chinese patterns. Number 12 is the **Tibetan Jewelry & Tea Bar,** where you can stop for a drink in the airy back room and browse their collection of Tibetan bracelets, rings, and clothing. ⏱ *20 min.*

Even the waterways sometimes get crowded at Yinding Qiao.

⑪ Drum Tower. We highly recommend the drumming performances held daily from 9 to 11:30am and 1:30 to 5pm underneath the bright yellow tile roof of the looming Drum Tower. *See p 12, bullet ④.*

⑫ Excuse Café. Just east of the back entrance of the Drum Tower is this cozy cafe serving excellent espressos. *68 Zhonglou Wan Hutong.* ☎ *010/6401-9867. $.*

A performance at the Drum Tower.

Wangfujing

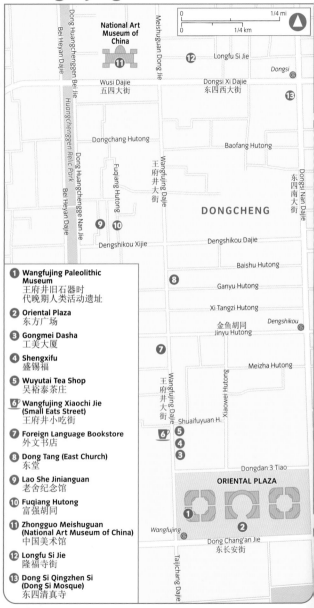

National Art Museum of China

Dong Huangchenggen Bei Jie

Bei Heyan Dajie

Meishuguan Dong Jie

11

Longfu Si Jie

Dongsi

Wusi Dajie
五四大街

Dongsi Xi Dajie
东四西大街

12

13

Huangchenggen Relic Park

Dongchang Hutong

Bei Heyan Dajie

Dong Huangchenggen Nan Jie

Dong Huangchenggen Bei Jie

Baofang Hutong

Wangfujing Dajie
王府井大街

Dongsi Nan Dajie
东四南大街

DONGCHENG

Fuqiang Hutong

9 **10**

Dengshikou Xijie

Dengshikou Dajie

Baishu Hutong

8

Ganyu Hutong

Xi Tangzi Hutong

Jinyu Hutong
金鱼胡同

Dengshikou

7

Meizha Hutong

Wangfujing Dajie
王府井大街

Xiaowei Hutong

6 **5**
4
3

Shuaifuyuan H.

Dongdan 3 Tiao

ORIENTAL PLAZA

1 **2**

Wangfujing

Dong Chang'an Jie
东长安街

Taijichang Dajie

Wangfujing has served as Beijing's traditional commercial heart since the end of the Qing dynasty, when the royal family fell on hard times and sold its silver to the neighborhood pawn-shops. Hipper commercial areas have sprung up around town, but Wangfujing contains the best pedestrian-friendly mix of historic sites, museums, kitschy Chinese shops, and outposts of Western consumerism—everything from Nike to Tiffany & Co. START: **Subway to Wangfujing, exit A.**

① Wangfujing Palaeolithic Museum. Construction workers struck animal skeletons and tools dating back 24,000 years when they were building the Oriental Plaza shopping mall. The government decided to commemorate the finding with this small, simple museum in the basement of an ultra modern shopping complex. The coolest thing is the exposed dirt floor, which shows pieces of embedded stones, bone tools, and animal fossils. 🕐 *15 min. 1 Dong Chang'an Jie.* ☎ *010/8518-6306. Admission ¥10. Daily 10am–4pm. Subway: Wangfujing, exit A.*

Jade at Gongmei Dasha.

A display at the Wangfujing Palaeolithic Museum.

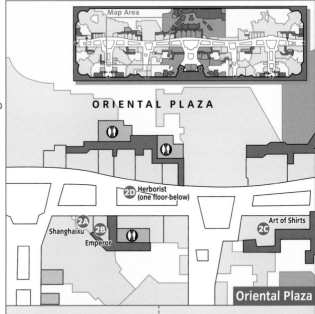

ORIENTAL PLAZA

Herborist (one floor-below) 2D

Art of Shirts 2C

Shanghaixu 2A 2B Emperor

Oriental Plaza

② Oriental Plaza. From the Wangfujing Paleolithic Museum, an escalator leads to the basement of one of Beijing's busiest malls. Critics wrongly predicted that this high-end mall would fail when it opened. Although the critics were right that former residents—evicted so that developers could build Oriental Plaza—can't afford to shop here, plenty of nouveau riche Chinese can. We tend to skip the familiar American and European brand-name stores, and hit the more unusual Chinese shops. The mall also boasts a good basement-level cinema and food court. **2A Shanghaixu,** at AA10, has a large selection of *qipaos*, traditional tight-fitting, high-collared Chinese dresses. If they don't have anything you like, you can get one made to order. Next door, **2B Emperor** has a nice assortment of embroidered napkins and housewares. A few shops down at AA20, **2C Art of Shirts** boasts a nice collection of buttondown and casual shirts for men and women. **2D The Herborist,** at EE05, carries a line of traditional Chinese medicine toiletries. We swear by their antidandruff shampoo. ⏱ *30 min. 1 Dong Chang'an Jie.* ☎ *010/8518-6573. Daily 9am–9:30pm.*

③ Gongmei Dasha. At this large jade store, you're guaranteed to get the real thing, rather than the colored glass you might find elsewhere. Bargain down to a third of the marked price. ⏱ *15 min. 200 Wangfujing Dajie.* ☎ *010/6528-8866. Daily 9:30am–9:30pm.*

④ Shengxifu. Established in 1912, this famed hat shop is the place to get your proletarian Mao cap or a furry hat with earflaps decorated with Communist red stars. ⏱ *10 min. 196 Wangfujing Dajie.* ☎ *010/6525-4752. Daily 8:30am–9pm.*

⑤ Wuyutai Tea Shop. The second floor of this quality tea shop has an interesting exhibition of tea culture, including a collection of teapots, and a lively teahouse. ⏱ *15 min. 186 Wangfujing Dajie.* ☎ *010/ 6525-4961. Daily 8:30am–9pm.*

⑥ Wangfujing Xiaochi Jie (Small Eats Street). These are our favorite stalls in town for street food. Don't be afraid to try the lamb skewers or the squid on the stick— though they may look suspect, they are scrumptious! *No phone. $.*

Skewers for sale on "Small Eats Street."

⑦ Foreign Language Bookstore. This aptly named store is one of Beijing's best foreign-language bookstores. On the ground level, you'll find a decent collection of fiction and nonfiction, Chinese cookbooks, maps, and travel guides. ⏱ *15 min. 235 Wangfujing Dajie.* ☎ *010/6512-6903. Daily 9:30am–9:30pm.*

⑧ Dong Tang (East Church). Also known as St. Joseph's Cathedral, this gray Gothic structure was built in 1655, toppled by an earthquake in 1720, gutted by a fire in 1807, and razed during the Boxer Rebellion of 1900. Rebuilt in 1904, it went through major renovations in 2000. Aside from devout Catholics, the

church attracts punk teenagers who skateboard in the outdoor square. If you're feeling a little tired, you're very close to the Donghua Jiankang Huisuo Massage Center (see "Pamper Yourself," p 46). ⏱ *10 min. 74 Wangfujing Dajie.* ☎ *010/6524-0634. Sun services at 6:30, 7, 8am; Mon–Sat services at 6:30 & 7am.*

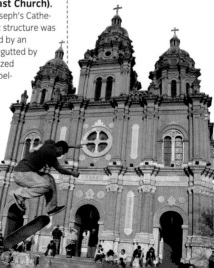

Skateboarding in front of Dong Tang.

Lao She Jinianguan.

9 Lao She Jinianguan. Across the street from the Donghua Jiank-ang Huisuo Massage Center (see "Pamper Yourself," below) are two narrow lanes. Take the lane on the left to reach this memorial hall to Lao She, one of China's most famous writers. When Lao She

returned to a newly Communist China in 1950, then-premier Zhou Enlai gave Lao She this courtyard residence in the hope that he would write propaganda novels for the new government. But he never turned out another famous novel, and he drowned himself during the Cultural Revolution. 🕐 *15 min. 19 Fengfu Hutong.* ☎ *010/6514-2612. Free admission. Daily 9am–4pm.*

10 Fuqiang Hutong. Retracing your steps back to the street, take the right alley, immodestly named "Rich and Powerful Alley." Note the finely carved roof lintels with Buddhist swastikas (an ancient symbol

Pamper Yourself

One of the things we love about living in Beijing is being able to indulge in inexpensive spa treatments that cost a fortune in the West. If you've done a walking tour or two, you more than deserve a visit to one of Beijing's masseuses.

The **Donghua Jiankang Huisuo Massage Center** offers 1-hour full-body and foot massages for ¥88 each. You can also try cupping, in which hot glass jars are used to suck out bad energy from your back, leaving funny-looking red welts. The massage center is on the second floor of the Donghua Hotel (32 Dengshikou Xi Jie; ☎ 010/6525-7531, ext. 3201).

Bodhi (17 Gongti Bei Lu; ☎ 010/6417-9595) is our favorite massage retreat. The hallways, decorated with Southeast Asian touches, lead to private rooms, where top-notch masseuses rub away knots in our backs. The spa offers traditional Chinese foot massages, body massages, Thai massages, and nail treatments. Complimentary drinks and snacks are served during and after your treatment.

With a convenient location near the Forbidden City, **Dragonfly** (Sanlitun Nan Lu Ground floor of the Eastern Inn, north gate of Chaoyang Hospital; ☎ 010/6593-6066), features a dark, serene interior and offers treatments similar to Bodhi, but without the snacks.

Head to the **Spa at the Ritz-Carlton** (1 Jinchengfang Dong Jie, Xicheng District; ☎ 010/6601-6666) if you're looking to splurge. The Ritz offers everything from facials to massages to pedicures, and you'll have access to their luxurious sauna and steam room before and after your treatment. The intimate rooms for two with candlelight are particularly romantic.

of good fortune) and the lotus-emblazoned door piers at number 18. While the rectangular door pier indicates that the residents weren't officials (their houses were marked by circular door piers), they must have been well-off to be able to afford skilled stonemasons. Party General Secretary Zhao Ziyang, who was ousted during the Tian'anmen massacre, lived at number 3 under house arrest until his death in January 2005. ⏲ *15 min.*

⓫ **Zhongguo Meishuguan (National Art Museum of China).** This museum has a good permanent collection of Chinese oil paintings and hosts international exhibitions curated by the likes of New York's Guggenheim Museum. ⏲ *60 min. 1 Wusi Dajie.* ☎ *010/8403-3500. www.namoc.org. Admission ¥20. Daily 9am–5pm (4pm last entry).*

⓬ **Longfu Si Jie.** In this small alley you'll find bargain clothes, music, and street food that make an interesting contrast to the bustle and commercial flair of Wangfujing. ⏲ *15 min.*

Shopping for fruit in Longfu Si Jie.

⓭ **Dong Si Qingzhen Si (Dong Si Mosque).** One of Beijing's oldest mosques, Dong Si Qingzhen Si has been around since the 14th century. The second courtyard is especially serene—a nice place to unwind and rest your feet. ⏲ *10 min. 13 Dongsi Nan Dajie.* ☎ *010/ 6525-7824. Admission ¥10. Daily sunrise–sunset.*

Take a break in the courtyard at Dong Si Qingzhen Si.

Liulichang

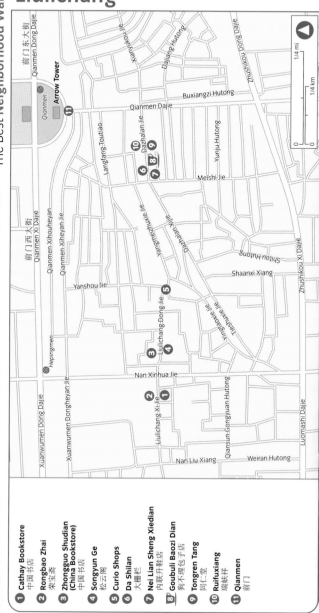

1 **Cathay Bookstore**
中国书店

2 **Rongbao Zhai**
荣宝斋

3 **Zhongguo Shudian (China Bookstore)**
中国书店

4 **Songyun Ge**
松云阁

5 **Curio Shops**

6 **Da Shilan**
大栅栏

7 **Nei Lian Sheng Xiedian**
内联升鞋店

8 **Goubuli Baozi Dian**
狗不理包子店

9 **Tongren Tang**
同仁堂

10 **Ruifuxiang**
瑞蚨祥

11 **Qianmen**
前门

Named for a factory that once churned out glazed roof tiles, Liulichang is a charming, chaotic mess of alleys brimming with life. While much of Beijing has been torn down to make way for monolithic skyscrapers and wide avenues, this is one of the few areas of town that has remained as it was at the turn of the 20th century. START: **Heping Men Metro station.**

1 Cathay Bookstore. This bookstore contains a great range of art materials, from ink stones (a mound of ink that can be wetted to use for calligraphy) to name chops and paper cuts, for reasonable prices. ⏱ *15 min. 18 Liulichang Xi Jie.* ☎ *010/6301-7678. Daily 9am–6:30pm.*

2 Rongbao Zhai. The most renowned art shop in China is flanked by the world's largest ink stone. The woodblock prints, copies of famous calligraphy, and historic paintings aren't cheap, but you're paying for the quality and cachet. ⏱ *15 min. 19 Liulichang Xi Jie.* ☎ *010/6303-5279. Daily 9am–5:30pm.*

3 Zhongguo Shudian (China Bookstore). Here you'll find a wide range of books on Chinese art, architecture, and literature. ⏱ *10 min. 115 Liulichang Dong Jie.* ☎ *010/ 6303-6694. Daily 9am–6pm.*

4 Songyun Ge. Just east of Zhongguo Shudian is this tiny shop, founded in 1903, with a marvelous collection of antiquarian books. *104 Liulichang Dong Jie.* ☎ *010/6303-1446. Daily 9am–6:30pm.*

5 Curio Shops. Continuing east, Liulichang Dong Jie peters out into a series of touristy shops that sell Buddhist statues, ceramics, and reproductions of Tang dynasty horses and emperors. Most of the street contains shops that sell the same knickknacks, but number 71 sells good chrysanthemum and green tea, and number 58 carries quality antiques and secondhand goods like grandfather clocks and jewelry. Just before number 65, turn right down an alley marked with a gate bafflingly labeled PRADIPRION SCULPTURE and follow the signs that say ANTIQUE CARPETS to 54 Dong Bei Yun Hutong. Here, a couple sells

Brushes for sale at the curio shops along Liulichang Dong Jie.

beautiful, antique Mongolian and Tibetan carpets (some made of camel hair) out of their small courtyard living room. Number 28 Liulichang Dong Lu sells elegant gray-green celadon teapots and vases.

6 Da Shilan. This bustling, pedestrian-only street is flanked by some of Beijing's oldest retailers; we've described our favorites just below.

7 Nei Lian Sheng Xiedian. On the right is this famous shoe store where you can see cobblers demonstrating their trade. The traditional cloth and delicately hand-embroidered women's shoes are worn by elders and hipsters alike. ⏲ *15 min. 34 Da Shilan.* ☎ *010/6301-4863. Daily 9:30am–8pm.*

8 Goubuli Baozi Dian. We're not sure why the dogs won't touch them (as the catchy moniker "goubuli" implies), but people certainly love the steamed buns sold by the steamer basket at this bustling, somewhat grungy restaurant. We prefer the ¥22 buns stuffed with wild vegetables and pork (ask for the yeshu bao) to the original pork-flavored buns. *29 Da Shilan.* ☎ *010/ 6315-2389. $.*

9 Tongren Tang. Beijing's most celebrated Chinese-medicine pharmacy was established in 1669. In the western wing, you can make an appointment to see a Chinese-medicine doctor, while in the main hall people of all ages—from youthful 20-somethings to senior citizens pushing ancient-looking wooden carts—browse the medicine counters. On the second floor, precious ginseng root that was harvested 80 years ago in Manchuria sells for a

A cobbler sewing shoes at Nei Lian Sheng Xiedian.

staggering ¥680,000. ⏲ *15 min. 29–31 Da Shilan.* ☎ *010/6353-3338. Daily 8am–7:30pm.*

10 Ruifuxiang. On the left is the steel baroque facade of a long established fabric store that once supplied silk to the Qing dynasty royalty. The company brochure claims that one of the first Chinese flags raised by Chairman Mao was also made from Ruifuxiang fabric. ⏲ *15 min. 5 Da Shilan.* ☎ *010/6303-5313. Daily 10am–7:30pm.*

11 Qianmen. Walking up the avenue, past the Front Gate (Zhengyang Men), take the roadway underpass to Qianmen, a towering remnant of the old city wall. Emperors once passed through Qianmen on their annual procession from the Forbidden City to the Temple of Heaven. The tower boasts excellent views of Tian'anmen Square and hosts a photographic exhibition of Old Beijing. Just south of the tower is a bustling new promenade that was finished just after the 2008 Olympic Games, boasting all kinds of international brands, from Starbucks to H&M. ⏲ *15 min. No phone. Admission ¥10. Daily 8:30am–4pm.* ●

Shopping Best Bets

Best **Place for Chinese Minority Costumes, Jewelry & Chairman Mao Memorabilia**
★★ Panjiayuan Jiuhuo Shichang, *Panjiayuan Lu (p 65)*

Best Place to **Haggle over Pirated Goods**
Yashow, *58 Gongti Bei Lu (p 66)*

Best **Young Designer**
★★ Lu 12.28, *81 Sanlitun Bei Lu (p 60)*

Most **Unique Toys**
Bannerman, *38 Guozijian (p 68)*

Best **Electronics**
Zhongguan Cun, *1 Zhongguan Cun Dajie (p 58)*

Best **Teapots & Teacups**
Spin, *6 Fangyuan Xilu (p 68)*

Best **Chinese Antique Furniture**
★ Gaobeidian, *Gaobeidian Gujiaju Jie (p 63)*

Best **Carpets**
★ Torana, *Kempinski Hotel (p 58)*

Best **Place to Get a Tailored Qipao**
Third floor of Yashow, *58 Gongti Bei Lu (p 66)*

Most Established **Contemporary Art Gallery**
Red Gate Gallery, *Dongbianmen Watchtower (p 57)*

Best **Photo Gallery**
Three Shadows Photography Art Centre, *155 Caochangdi (p 57)*

Best **High-Quality, Bargain Pearls**
Hongqiao Shichang, *16 Hongqiao Lu (p 65)*

Best **Designer Discounts**
Zoo Market, *in front of the Beijing Zoo (p 62)*

Best **Tea Shop**
Maliandao, *Maliandao Lu (p 67)*

Best **Souvenir Beijing T-Shirt**
Plastered T-shirt Shop, *61Nanluo Guxiang (p 60)*

Best **Place to Find Street Shoes Worthy of an Asian Hip-Hop Star**
★ Deal, *280 Gulou Dong Dajie (p 59)*

Best **Place for One-Stop Gift Shopping for Your Extended Family**
★ Esydragon, *19-1 Nanluoguxiang (p 63)*

Teapots and cups for sale in Beijing range from the traditional to the contemporary. Previous page: Merchandise for sale at the Panjiayuan market.

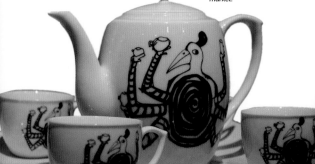

Embassy Area Shopping

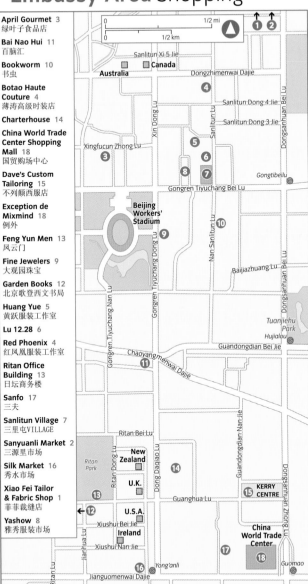

April Gourmet 3
绿叶子食品店

Bai Nao Hui 11
百脑汇

Bookworm 10
书虫

Botao Haute Couture 4
薄涛高级时装店

Charterhouse 14

China World Trade Center Shopping Mall 18
国贸购物中心

Dave's Custom Tailoring 15
不列颠西服店

Exception de Mixmind 18
例外

Feng Yun Men 13
凤云门

Fine Jewelers 9
大观园珠宝

Garden Books 12
北京歌登西文书局

Huang Yue 5
黄跃服装工作室

Lu 12.28 6

Red Phoenix 4
红凤凰服装工作室

Ritan Office Building 13
日坛商务楼

Sanfo 17
三夫

Sanlitun Village 7
三里屯VILLAGE

Sanyuanli Market 2
三源里市场

Silk Market 16
秀水市场

Xiao Fei Tailor & Fabric Shop 1
菲菲裁缝店

Yashow 8
雅秀服装市场

Beijing Shopping

Wangfujing Shopping

0   1/4 mi
0   1/4 km

Dengshikou Xi Jie

Dengshikou Dajie

东四南大街 Dongsi Nan Dajie

Baishu Hutong

Bei Heyan Dajie

Dong Huangchengge Nan Jie

王府井大街 Wangfujing Dajie

Ganyu Hutong

Xi Tangzi Hutong

金鱼胡同 Jinyu Hutong

Dengshikou

Donghuamen Dajie

Dong'anmen Dajie

Huangchengen Relic Park

Meizha Hutong

Xiaowei Hutong

Daruanfu Hutong

Shuaifuyuan H.

Nan Heyan Dajie

Dongdan 3 Tiao

ORIENTAL PLAZA

Hualong Jie

Wangfujing

Dong Chang'an Jie
东长安街

Zhengyi Lu

Taijichang Dajie

①②③④⑤⑥⑦

Gongmei Dasha 6 工美大厦	**Shengxifu** 5 盛锡福
Herborist 7 佰草集	**Tom Lee** 2 通利乐器行
The Malls at Oriental Plaza 7 东方新天地	**Wangfujing Foreign Language Bookstore** 1 王府井外文书店
Shanghai Tang 7 上海滩	**Wuyutai Tea Shop** 4 吴裕泰茶庄
Shanghai Xu 7 上海徐	**Xin Zhong Guo Kid's Stuff** 3 新中国儿童用品商店

Beijing Shopping A to Z

Antiques

★ **Guang Han Tang** CHAOYANG   A run-down warehouse converted into an elegant courtyard, this emporium full of Tibetan trunks, antique carpets, and rosewood furniture is worth the long trip if you've got serious cash. *Caochangdi (call for more specific directions).* ☎ *010/8456-7943. No credit cards. Map p 54.*

★★ **Panjiayuan Jiuhuo Shichang** CHAOYANG   See "Markets & Bazaars," later in this chapter.

Art, Contemporary

★ **Faurschou** CHAOYANG   This high-caliber Copenhagen gallery, located in the 798 Art District, represents top international and Chinese artists, and the airy, cavernous space is well-designed to view its large, pricey exhibitions. *2 Jiuxianqiao Lu.* ☎ *010/5978 9316. www.faurschou.com/beijing. AE, MC, V. Map p 54.*

★ **Pekin Fine Arts** CHAOYANG   Promoting established Asian artists, this gallery, located in the Caochangdi art district, caters to high-end art collectors and museums, but is worth a tour even if you are a casual browser of art. Pair it with a visit to Three Shadows, listed below, and dip in to the other galleries in the area. *241 Caochangdi.* ☎ *010/5127-3220. www.pekinfinearts. com. AE, MC, V.*

Panjiayuan has jewelry, ceramics, Cultural Revolution memorabilia, and more.

If you're serious about art, two districts should be on your checklist: 798, which is featured in the previous chapter (p 21), and Caochangdi, where Pekin Fine Arts and Three Shadows Photography Art Centre (see below) are located. Caochangdi has a more exclusive feel, while 798 attracts a lot of young, casual shoppers interested in shops that sell clothing and knickknacks that surround the galleries. Another point to consider is that 798 is quite walkable, whereas the distances between galleries at Caochangdi are larger, so you might think about renting a car and driver for the day if you're interested in Caochangdi.

★★ **Red Gate Gallery** CHAOYANG   The grandfather of art galleries in Beijing, Red Gate opened 1991 and continues to be a leader in the scene. Located in a watchtower that used to be part of the city wall, the gallery is worth a trip for its stunning architecture alone. *Dongbianmen Watchtower.* ☎ *010/6525-1005. www. redgategallery.com. AE, MC, V. Metro: Jianguomen. Map p 54.*

★ **Three Shadows Photography Art Centre** CHAOYANG   Specializing in photography by established and emerging Chinese artist, this is my favorite gallery in the city. With its long perimeter of walls, a beautiful courtyard, and a nice cafe on the premises, it's a place you can hang out for several hours and soak up its exhibitions. *155 Caochangdi. www.threeshadows.com.* ☎ *010/6432-2663. AE, MC, V.*

Arts & Crafts

Beijing Central Art Gallery & Cultural Village SHUNYI   This professional gallery has original (both traditional and contemporary) watercolors, oil paintings, and sculptures by Chinese artists. The staff is incredibly friendly and helpful. *50 Liangmaqiao Lu. Kempinski Hotel.* ☎ *010/6465-1396. www.bjcagallery.com. AE, MC, V. Map p 54.*

★★ Panjiayuan Jiuhuo Shichang CHAOYANG   See "Markets & Bazaars," later in this chapter.

★ Zaoyuang Artifact Shop XICHENG   For an intimate shopping experience, head to this cozy courtyard shop. They sell high-quality ceramic reproductions endorsed by research fellows from the Forbidden City museum. They also have calligraphy paintings by well-known Beijing calligraphers. *2 Zhuzhong Hutong, Jiugulou Dajie.* ☎ *010/8401-8867. No credit cards. Metro: Gulou. Map p 54.*

Carpets

★ Torana SHUNYI   It's a trek to get out here and the prices are high, but if you're looking for a premium carpet-shopping experience, this is the place to go. Torana's extensive selection of carpets prominently features works from Tibet, and the store is also a great resource if you're looking for information on how to select and clean carpets. *Europlaza Mall (Oulu Guangchang), 99 Fuxiang Lu, L110.* ☎ *010/8459-0785. AE, MC, V. Map p 54.*

★ Mr. Zhang's Carpets CHAOYANG   This friendly carpet dealer is a favorite among expats in Beijing. Two large dusty sheds are filled with beautiful woven works from western China and Central Asia. Be sure to bring cash and bargain to get cut-rate prices between ¥1,000 and ¥10,000. *Sanyuan Nan Xiao Jie (call for exact directions).* ☎ *139/0100-5150. No credit cards. Metro: Nongzhanguan. Map p 54.*

Chinese Medicine & Pharmacies

Beijing International SOS Clinic CHAOYANG   With the number of fake Western medicines on the Chinese market, your best bet is to go to SOS for its selection of imported medicine. *Ste. 105, Wing 1, Kunsha Bldg., 16 Xinyuanli Lu.* ☎ *010/6462-9112. AE, MC, V. Metro: Liangmahe. Map p 54.*

Tongren Tang DONGCHENG   Beijing's most celebrated Chinese medicine pharmacy was established in 1669. In the western wing, you can make an appointment to see a Chinese- medicine doctor, while in the main hall people of all ages—from youthful 20-somethings to senior citizens pushing ancient-looking wooden carts—browse the medicine counters. On the second floor, precious ginseng root that was harvested 80 years ago in Manchuria sells for a staggering ¥680,000. *24 Da Shilan.* ☎ *010/6303-0221. No credit cards. Metro: Qianmen. Map 54.*

Electronics

Bai Nao Hui CHAOYANG   Though it's a four-story mess of stalls, Bai Nao Hui is centrally located, and the vendors take care of our gadget cravings, selling everything from the tiniest MP3 players to the sleekest digital cameras. Go with a Mandarin speaker, ask about warranties, and get a receipt for big-ticket purchases. *Chaowai Dajie 10.* ☎ *010/6599-5947. Metro: Chaoyang Men. Map p 53.*

★ Zhongguan Cun HAIDIAN   Beware: You could spend days

The Bookworm.

weaving through several blocks' worth of stores here. A good place to start is **Hailong Shopping Mall,** a five-story mecca with familiar tenants like Lenovo and Sony selling assembled laptops and PCs, as well as independent dealers selling everything from motherboards to wireless headphones. The same rules apply here as at Bai Nao Hui above. *Zhongguan Cun Dajie.* ☎ *010/8266-3812. Metro: Zhongguancun. Map p 54.*

English-Language Books
★ **The Bookworm** CHAOYANG This cafe, which draws a big expat crowd, carries an excellent selection of contemporary novels, books on China, and popular magazines. We come for the books and the company, but avoid the lackluster food. *Bldg. 4, Nan Sanlitun Lu.* ☎ *010/ 6586-9507. www.beijingbookworm. com. MC, V. Metro: Gongtibeilu. Map p 53.*

Charterhouse CHAOYANG This bookstore has a nice selection of foreign magazines—*Elle, National Geographic,* and plenty of home decor monthlies. The book selection's not shabby either. *Store B107, The Place.* ☎ *010/6587-1328. AE,* *MC, DISC, V. Metro: Guanghualu. Map p 53.*

★ **Garden Books** CHAOYANG With a cafe downstairs, this quaint bookstore features a good collection of children's literature, cookbooks, and recent nonfiction and fiction. *44 Guanghua Lu* ☎ *010/6585-1435. www.gardenbooks.cn. AE, MC, V. Metro: Jianguomen. Map p 53.*

Wangfujing Foreign Languages Bookstore DONGCHENG A few years ago, China's strict censorship laws restricted the stock in this bookstore to Western classics. Nowadays, we're happy to find the latest bestsellers, novels by Haruki Murakami, and good biographies alongside classics by the likes of Jane Austen. *235 Wangfujing Dajie, Dongcheng Qu.* ☎ *010/6512-6903. AE, MC, V. Metro: Wangfujing. Map p 56.*

Fashion
★ **Deal** DONGCHENG We love this hip shoe store's too-cool-for-school attitude and wide range of street wear kickers. They stock international special-edition shoes by Ice Cream, Nike, and Adidas' Adicolor line, plus a handful of regional

Asian designs by Nike (mostly space-age looking stuff from Japan). *280 Gu Lou Dong Dajie.* ☎ *010/ 6402-8262. www.dealkicks.com. AE, MC, V. Metro: Gulou. Map p 54.*

Exception de Mixmind CHAOY-ANG   Southern Chinese designer Ma Ke's minimalist dresses and coats are pricey for the quality, but it can be worth a peek to see styles by a rising star of the Chinese fashion world. *China World Mall (see "Shopping Centers & Complexes," p 66).* ☎ *010/6505-2268. www. mixmind.com. AE, DISC, MC, V. Metro: Guomao. Map p 53.*

★★ **Lu 12.28** CHAOYANG   Lu Liu, the energetic young designer behind this brand, studied at Parsons in New York and Paris and creates well-cut feminine dresses, semi-casual wear, and professional clothes. Lu is often at the store and plies plenty of attention on her clients. *Nali Patio, 81 Sanlitun Bei Lu.* ☎ *010/5208-6105. www.lu1228.com. MC, V. Metro: Gongtibeilu. Map p 53.*

★ **Plastered T-Shirt Shop** DONGCHENG   This quirky little store run by an English/Canadian husband-and-wife team sells T-shirts with humorous, in-your-face slogans, like the label from Er Gou Tou, a cheap 112-proof grain alcohol, and a close-up of a Beijing subway ticket. *61 Nanlouguxiang St.* ☎ *139/1020-5721. www.plastered. com.cn. MC, V. Metro: Beixinqiao. Map p 54.*

Shanghai Tang CHAOYANG This Hong Kong–based international retailer is the ambassador for modern Chinese style. Their clothes feature luxurious knits and silks worked into innovative Chinese designs. *B1/F of the Grand Hyatt Beijing in Oriental Plaza (see "Shopping Centers & Complexes," p 66).* ☎ *010/8518-0898. www.shanghai tang.com. M, V. Metro: Wangfujing. Map p 56.*

★ **Woo** DONCHENG   If you're looking for wispy scarves or extremely soft cashmere wraps, head over to this cute little shop, run by a Shanghai designer, on a quaint, touristy alley in Beijing's old quarter. *110-1Nanlouguxiang. Map p 54.*

Lu Liu displaying one of her dresses at Lu 12.28.

Plastered T-Shirt Shop

☎ 010/6400-5395. www.shanghai woo.com. AE, MC, V. Metro: Zhangzizhonglu.

Custom-Made Chinese Fashion

★ **Botao Haute Couture** CHA-OYANG We love Botao's innovative designs and luxurious fabrics. They're like affordable couture; the store displays samples that you order and have tailored especially for you. *18 Dongzhimenwai Dajie (corner of Dongzhimenwai Dajie and Xindong Lu).* ☎ *010/6417-2472. AE, DISC, MC, V. Metro: Gongtibeilu. Map p 53.*

Feng Yun Men CHAOYANG This shop can custom embroider a qipao, the high-collared, tight-fitting traditional Chinese dress. *Shop 1006, Ritan Office Bldg., 15AGuanghua Lu, east of the south gate of Ritan Park, next to Schindlers.* ☎ *010/8563-0702. AE, MC. V. Metro: Guanghualu. Map p 53.*

★ **Huang Yue** CHAOYANG This Sichuan designer's whimsical, imperial dresses and coats attract a loyal French following. *Sanlitun (behind 3.3 Fashion Plaza).* ☎ *010/6417-1093. AE, MC, V. Metro: Gongtibeilu. Map p 53.*

Red Phoenix CHAOYANG Here, Tibetan-inspired qipaos can be custom made by the boutique's devout Buddhist designer. *30 Sanlitun Bei Lu, Bldg. 30.* ☎ *010/6416-4423. AE, MC, V. Metro: Gongtibeilu. Map p 53.*

Shanghai Xu DONGCHENG This store offers modern twists on familiar qipaos, like taking typical Chinese prints and pairing them with bright neon-pink piping or a flashy turquoise trim. *AA10 Oriental Plaza (see "Shopping Centers & Complexes," p 66).* ☎ *010/8518-6376. AE, MC, V. Metro: Wangfujing. Map p 56.*

Discount Fashion

★★ **Ritan Shangwu Lou (Ritan Office Building)** CHAOYANG Laundry, Max Mara, and BCBG, oh my! From the outside, Ritan Office Building looks like any other drab structure, but it is teeming with high-quality women's wear. Genuine sample pieces outweigh the fakes (a rule of thumb: if the designer tag has been snipped, you're probably getting the real deal. Our favorite store is 1008, for its excellent selection of dresses and outerwear. *15AGuanghua Lu, east of the south gate of Ritan Park, next to Schindlers.* ☎ *010/8561-9556. M, V (not all stores). Metro: Guanghualu. Map p 53.*

★ **Zoo Market** XICHENG   The main draw of this massive wholesale market is the insanely cheap prices you'll pay for what appears to be real Diane von Furstenberg dresses and Marc Jacobs tops. The downsides? It's a bit of a trek, sorting through the huge number of stalls is exhausting, and it's unlikely that there will be fitting rooms. Bring cash and wear tight-fitting clothes to make it easy to slip potential items on and off. Look for a series of nondescript buildings in front of the Beijing Zoo, hence the name of the market. *Beijing Dongwuyuan Zhoubian. No phone. No credit cards. Metro: Xizhimen. Map p 54.*

Food Markets

★ **April Gourmet** CHAOYANG   Beijing's most extensive grocery store for foreigners has all kinds of goodies you've been missing from home, including a great range of cheeses, coffee, and breads. A deli

A selection of fresh fish at Sanyuanli Market.

featuring ready-made salads and sushi makes it easy to pick up a quick lunch if you're on the go. *Xingfuzhong Lu, next to Lianbao Apartments.* ☎ *010/6417-7950.* ☎ *010/ 5208 6105. www.aprilgourmet.com. MC, V. Metro: Dongsisitiao. Map p 53.*

★ **Sanyuanli Market** CHAOYANG   This is a fabulous place to find fresh everything. The market supplies the foreign grocery stores and restaurants around town, so it's our favorite go-to place for feta cheese on the cheap, handfuls of fresh basil, or a couple of limes for a proper

A dress at Huang Yue.

cocktail. *Sanyuanli (opposite Jing-kelong Supermarket, west of Sanyuan Dongqiao). No credit cards. Metro: Nongzhanguan. Map p 53.*

Gifts & Souvenirs
★★ **Esydragon** DONGCHENG
This is one of my favorite places to pick up gifts for friends and family back home. They've got a great selection of children's toys, photo frames, mugs, and housewares, all with Chinese motifs. The goods they display are a couple of notches higher in quality than the stuff you'll find at the knockoff markets in town. *19–1 Nanluoguxiang.* ☎ *010/8401-1516. www.esydragon.cn. MC, V. Metro: Beixinqiao. Map p 54.*

Herborist DONGCHENG   This is a Chinese version of the Body Shop, with a twist. The body products here are made with Chinese tradi-tional medicine—and we swear by the antidandruff shampoo. *EE05 Ori-ental Plaza (see "Shopping Centers & Complexes," p 66).* ☎ *010/8518-6573. www.hearborist.com.cn. No credit cards. Metro: Wangfujing. Map p 56.*

★★ **Panjiayuan Jiuhuo Shichang** CHAOYANG   See "Mar-kets & Bazaars," p 65.

Shengxifu DONGCHENG   Estab-lished in 1912, this famed hat shop is the place to get your proletarian Mao cap or a furry hat with earflaps decorated with Communist red stars. *196 Wangfujing Dajie.* ☎ *010/6525-4752. V. Metro: Wangfujing. Map p 56.*

Yandai Alley DONGCHENG   This alleyway sells everything from reproductions of Cultural Revolution posters to delicate China tea sets. You can also buy some "for me" gifts at the cool clothing and statio-nery stores nearby. *Yandai Xiejie, off the west side of Di'anmenwai Dajie and south of the Drum Tower.*

A selection of hats at Shengxifu.

No credit cards. Metro: Gulou. Map p 54.

Housewares & Furnishings
★ **Gaobeidian Antique Furni-ture Village** CHAOYANG   This area features a 3km (1¾-mile) street stocked with stores that sell genu-ine antique, restored, and antique reproduction Chinese furniture. Most stores can arrange to ship items overseas. *Gaobeidian Gujiaju Cun. The main street is right before the railroad tracks. Map p 54.*

★ **Lost & Found**
DONGCHENG   Echoing the feel of Restoration Hardware, this lovely shop on a historic alley in Beijing near Lama Temple is worth a trip for its furniture, notebooks, ceramics, and T-shirts. You can also browse the cafes and shops nearby, including the Bannerman Toy Store (p 68). *42 Guozhijian.* ☎ *010/6401-1855. www.lost-and-found.cn. MC, V. Metro: Yonghe-gong. Map p 54.*

Bare-Bones Bargaining

Even after living in Beijing for several years, I still walk away from some transactions thinking: Did I just get the "foreigner" price? Certain markets will absolutely take advantage of tourists' willingness to pay higher prices. Unless you're shopping at malls or high-end retailers, you should be bargaining with salespeople for a better price. Here are some general guidelines to ensure a successful bargaining experience:

1. Aim to pay approximately 50% to 65% of the initial offering price.
2. *Do not* get upset. "Face" is a very important concept in Beijing. If you get angry at a salesperson, he or she may view it as a huge loss of face and refuse to deal with you.
3. Only engage in a bargaining session when you are committed to buying. Changing your mind after you and the vendor have settled on a price is considered extremely rude (vendors will lose face), and you will most likely find yourself on the receiving end of one very angry rant.
4. One technique to get prices down is to point out the flaws in the garment/item. Show the vendor how it is not of very good quality or let him know it doesn't quite fit you, so it cannot possibly be worth the price he is demanding. I am not a big fan of this technique and am more inclined to use technique number five, below.
5. Be complimentary. Let the salesperson know that whatever you're bargaining for is really nice, that the store has so many lovely things, and you really want to buy this particular thing, but it's just too expensive. If they could just bring the price down a couple of more notches, you would be happy to snatch it up.
6. Keep the idea of relative value in mind. I've been known to get so swept up in the moment that I've spent 20 minutes bargaining for an extra ¥10 discount, only to stop myself and realize that saving $1.30 is not worth the extra time, effort, and headache.

MaLiLian Furniture CHAOYANG
The armchairs and ottomans made by this European expatriate incorporate Chinese silk, Belgian lace, camel hair, and rabbit fur. *By appointment only. Jianwai SOHO, Suite 1606, Bldg. 14, 39 Dong Sanhuan Zhong Lu.* ☎ *0/137-0110-1406. www.malilian.com. No credit cards. Metro: Guomao. Map p 54.*

★★ Panjiayuan Jiuhuo Shichang CHAOYANG   See "Markets & Bazaars," below.

Jewelry

★★ Fine Jewelers CHAOYANG
A favorite in the expat community, this is the place to go if you're looking for custom- made jewelry. They're happy to accommodate your own designs and even have knockoffs of Tiffany and Cartier designs. It's great for gold and silver jewelry, though the quality of platinum is shaky. *Gongti Dong Lu, China View Bldg. No. 3, Room 306.*

Most of the pearls sold at Hongqiao Shichang are genuine, though low quality.

☎ 010/6592-7118. AE, MC, V. Metro: Gongtibeilu. Map p 53.

Gongmei Dasha DONGCHENG At this large jade store, you're guaranteed to get the real thing, rather than the colored glass you might find elsewhere. Bargain down to a third of the marked price. *See p 44, bullet ❸. 200 Wangfujing Dajie.* ☎ 010/6528-8866. V. Metro: Wangfujing. Map p 56.

Hongqiao Pearl Market CHONGWEN Pearls are one of the many items sold at this market. Also available are Cultural Revolution kitsch, typical brand-name clothing, luggage, and watches. The pearls are a big draw, however, and are sold in every size, shape, and color, with a similarly vast range in price. *9 Tiantan Lu.* ☎ 010/6713-3354. No credit cards. Metro: Tiantandongmen. Map p 54.

★ Yin Shu + EA West CHAOYANG We love artist Man Kaihui's unique, industrial-looking jewelry. This boutique also sells locally

designed sweaters and dresses. *798 Art District, 2 Jiuxianqiao Lu.* ☎ 010/6437-3432. MC, V. Map p 54.

Markets & Bazaars
★★ Panjiayuan Jiuhuo Shichang CHAOYANG This is the mother ship for all your China gift shopping needs. This large outdoor market is filled with Chinese curios, paintings, calligraphy, jewelry, Chinese revolution memorabilia, ethnic clothes, ceramics, and furniture. Come early in the morning to find the best stuff; vendors start to leave around 4pm. *South side of Panjiayuan Lu. No credit cards. Map p 54.*

Silk Market (Xiushui Jie) CHAOYANG This place answers the question most Beijing visitors can't help but ask: "Where's the fakes market?" It is tempting to think—but extremely unlikely—that these items are the real deal, so bargain hard. We suggest you stick to the interesting Sino gifts, such as silk scarves and name chops (a stamp made of wood or jade engraved with the Chinese name of your choice). *Corner of Jianguomenwai*

Tom Lee.

Dajie and Xiushui Dong Jie. ☎ 010/6501-8811. No credit cards. Metro: Yong'anli. Map p 53.

Yashow Market (Yaxiu Fuzhuang Shichang) CHAOYANG

Yashow follows the same formula as the Silk Market, but is bigger and has better tailors (located on the 3rd floor). 58 Gongti Bei Lu. ☎ 010/6415-1726. No credit cards. Metro: Gongtibeilu. Map p 53.

Musical Instruments
Tom Lee (Hong Sheng)

DONGCHENG This is a department store for musical instruments; they have pretty much everything. One cool item is the Freehand Music Pad (¥14,500), a digital notebook that replaces sheet music. 201 Wangfujing Dajie (inside Lisheng Sports Shopping Mall). ☎ 010/6525-6255. MC, V. Metro: Wangfujing. Map p 56.

Zhiyin Wanli Instruments

DONGCHENG This store carries enough to start your own rock band: guitars, basses, and amps. If you can't find what you're looking for here, continue west on the main street, where you'll run into several drum, bass, and guitar dudes. Southeast corner of Jiaodaokou intersection. ☎ 010/8403-7683. No credit cards. Metro: Beixinqiao. Map p 54.

A shirt at Dave's Custom Tailoring.

Shopping Centers & Complexes
kids China World Trade Center Shopping Mall (Guomao Shangcheng) CHAOYANG The

big-label designer stores such as Prada and Gucci are the same as

they are anywhere, but this mall is also home to at least one original Chinese designer, Exception de Mixmind (p 60), and you can take the kids for a spin on the ice rink. 1 Jianguomenwai Dajie. ☎ 010/6505-2288. www.cwtc.com.cn. AE, V, MC. Metro: Guomao. Map p 53.

The Malls at Oriental Plaza (Dongfang Xintian Di)

DONGCHENG This is Western-style consumerism at its best, with everything from Nike to Tiffany & Co. A few original Chinese shops stand out from the others (see the Wangfujing walking tour in chapter 3). 1 Dongchang'an Jie. ☎ 010/8518-6363. www.orientalplaza.com. AE, MC, V. Metro: Wangfujing. Map p 56.

Sanlitun Village CHAOYANG A little piece of Southern California right in the middle of Beijing, this shopping mall has become all the rage with its central plaza with a water fountain, a movie theater, and American outposts such as Cold Stone and Columbia Sports. But if you didn't come to Beijing for all that, head a few steps north to Nali Patio, where you'll find boutiques with more Asian flavor. Sanlitun Bei Lu. ☎ 010/6417-6110. www.sanlitunvillage.com. AE, MC, V. Metro: Gongtibeilu. Map p 53.

Shin Kong Place

CHAOYANG Since opening in 2008, this mall has been considered the best in town, with a large selection of midrange to luxury international brands. You won't find much Chinese character to the place though, except for in the lively food-court basement. The mall also features some good

Chinese restaurants on the sixth floor. *87 Jianguo Lu.* ☎ *010/6530-5888. AE, MC, V. Metro: Dawanglu. Map p 54.*

Silk, Fabric & Tailors

Dave's Custom Tailoring CHAOYANG   This is one of the few tailors that has high-quality, imported fabrics, but the prices are pretty steep, upwards of ¥4,000. *104 Kerry Center, 1 Guanghua Lu.* ☎ *010/8529-9433. www.tailordave.com. AE, MC, V. Metro: Guomao. Map p 53.*

Ruifuxiang DONGCHENG   Behind a steel baroque facade is this long-established fabric store that once supplied silk to the Qing dynasty royalty. The company brochure claims that one of the first Chinese flags raised by Chairman Mao was made from Ruifuxiang fabric. *5 Da Shilan.* ☎ *010/6303-5313. AE, MC, V. Metro: Qianmen. Map p 54.*

You'll find much higher quality teas at Maliandao than you will in the West.

Xiao Fei Tailor and Fabric Shop CHAOYANG   Located close to the embassy district, this tailor has developed a loyal following among the diplomatic crowd. Xiao Fei (the main tailor) and her assistants all do excellent work, but it will probably take several fittings to get things just right. *Bldg. 1–103, 35 Xinyuan Jie.* ☎ *010/8455-1939. No credit cards. Metro: Nongzhanguan. Map p 53.*

Sporting Goods: Clothing & Equipment

Decathalon CHAOYANG   A place to get the real stuff. This is basically an outlet of the sporty French retailer. It has everything for the outdoors at significantly lower prices than what you would find back home. *195 Dongsihuan Zhonglu (corner of Nanmofang Lu and East Fourth Ring Road.).* ☎ *010/8777-8788. www.decathlon.com.cn. MC, V. Map p 54.*

★ **Sanfo** CHAOYANG   Prices for camping and hiking equipment here are rock bottom. We've bought gloves, climbing ropes, and clothes here. It's also a great place to get advice on local hiking spots. *1/F Jinshiqiao Dasha, Jianguomenwai Da Jie.* ☎ *010/6507-9298. www.sanfo. com. AE, MC, V. Metro: Guomao. Map p 53.*

Tea & Teapots

★ **Maliandao** XUANWU   You'll find tea shops galore, but don't expect anything cute or quaint: This is a Chinese clearinghouse for tea, and huge emporiums with hundreds of little stalls line a wide street. Stop by **Gu Yen Fan,** *3rd floor, stall 28, just south of the Carrefour Supermarket, 11 Maliandao Lu.* ☎ *0/136-8304-5808,* whose young owner, Mr. Liu, sells Lapsong Suchong by the kilo (and smaller amounts) from the mountains of Anhui Province.

Spin Ceramics (Fangyuan Xilu) CHAOYANG   Modern twists on the classic mug. Everything is a little offbeat and crooked, such as teacups with slight bends and blob-shaped saucers, but it's all done in a very funky style. *6 Fangyuan Xilu.* ☎ *010/6437-8649. AE, DISC, MC, V. Map p 54.*

Wuyutai Tea Shop DONGCHENG   The second floor of this quality tea shop has an interesting exhibition of tea culture, including a collection of teapots, and a lively teahouse. See p 45, bullet ⑤. *186 Wangfujing Dajie.* ☎ *010/6525-4961. MC, V. Metro: Wangfujing. Map p 56.*

Toys

★ **Bannerman Tang's Toys and Crafts** DONGCHENG   This store, run by fifth-generation toy maker Tang Yujie, is stocked with a delightful collection of figurines, paper lanterns, and other childish delights made from wood, clay, paper, and cloth. *38 Guozijian.* ☎ *010/8404-7179. No credit cards. Metro: Yonghegong. Map p 54.*

Xin Zhong Guo Kid's Stuff DONGCHENG   In stark contrast to the intimate family-run Bannerman Tang's toy store, this toy store celebrates all things commercial. Some just-in-China toys, such as puzzles and magic tricks, are mixed in with the mainstream stuff. *168 Wangfujing Dajie.* ☎ *010/6528-1774. No credit cards. Metro: Wangfujing. Map p 56.*

Buying Pearls

Most of the pearls on sale at Hong Qiao Shichang are genuine, although of too low quality to be sold in Western jewelry shops. However, some fakes are floating around. To test if the pearls you want to buy are real, try any one of the following:

Nick the surface with a sharp blade (the color should be uniform within and without)

Rub the pearl across your teeth (this should make a grating sound)

Scrape the pearl on a piece of glass (real pearls leave a mark)

Pass it through a flame (fake pearls turn black, real ones don't)

Oddly, vendors are generally willing to let you carry out these tests, and may even help, albeit with bemused faces. If you'd rather not bother (most don't), assume the worst, shop for fun, and spend modestly. ●

Whimsical figurines at Bannerman Tang's.

Dining **Best Bets**

Best **Place to Set Your Tongue on Fire**
★ Sichuan Provincial Restaurant $ 5 Gongyuan Toutiao, Jianguomen Nei Dajie (p 84)

Best **Northern-Style Dumplings**
★ Xian'r Lao Man $ 252 Andingmen Nei Dajie (p 85)

Wackiest **Decor**
Lan $$$ 12 Jianguomenwai Dajie Yi (p 80)

Best for **Vegetarians**
★ Pure Lotus $$ 10 Nongzhanguan Nan Lu (p 83)

Best **Pizza & Beer**
The Tree $$ Nan 43, Sanlitun Beijie Chaoyang (p 85)

Best **Brunch**
★★ The Orchard $$$ Hegezhuang Cun, Cuigezhuang Xiang (p 83)

Best **Noodles**
★ Noodle Loft $$ 20 Xi Dawang Lu, Chaoyang (p 82)

Best and Most Unusual **Desserts**
★ Bellagio $$ 35 Xiaoyun Lu (p 76)

Most **Romantic**
★ Courtyard $$$$$ 95 Donghua Men Dajie (p 77); and Dali Courtyard $$$ 67 Xiaojingchang Hutong (p 78)

Best **Peking Duck**
★★★ Da Dong $$ 22 Dongsi Shi Tiao (p 77)

Best **Hot Pot (Chinese Fondue)**
★ Ding Ding Xiang $$ 2/F, Yuanjia International Apartments, Dongzhimenwai, Dongzhong Jie (p 78)

Best **Lunch Deal in Classy Digs**
★ Mosto $$ (p 81)

Best **Hotel Restaurant**
★ Bei (p 76) or ★ Sureño (p 84) $$$ Opposite House, 11 Sanlitun Bei Lu

Best for **Shanghai Soup Dumplings**
★★ Din Tai Fung $$ 24 Xinyuanli Zhong Jie (p 78)

Best **Flipping-Freshest Sushi**
★★ Yotsuba $$$ 2 Xinyuanli Zhong Jie (p 86)

Most **Panoramic View of Quintessential Beijing**
★ Capital M $$$ 2 Qianmen Buxing Jie (p 78)

Best **Splurge**
★★ Maison Boulud $$$$ 23 Qianmen Dong Da Jie (p 81)

Best **Dim Sum**
★★ Le Galerie $ Ritan Park South Gate (p 80); and Lei Garden $$ 89 Jinbao Jie (p 80)

A bowl of noodles at Noodle Loft. Previous page: A dish of fruit at Luce.

Houhai Lake Area **Dining**

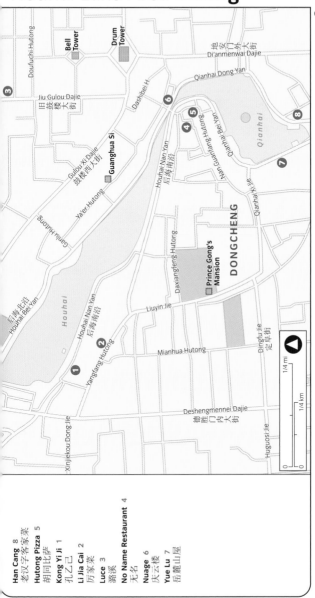

Han Cang 8
老汉字客家菜

Hutong Pizza 5
胡同比萨

Kong Yi Ji 1
孔乙己

Li Jia Cai 2
厉家菜

Luce 3
路谠溪

No Name Restaurant 4
无名

Nuage 6
庆云楼

Yue Lu 7
岳麓山屋

Sanlitun **Dining**

Bei 6
北

Bellagio 2
鹿港小镇

Element Fresh 9
新元素

Feiteng Yuxiang 1
沸腾鱼乡

Green T. House 3
紫云轩

Karaiya Spice House 8

Mosto 7

Sureño 6

Three Guizhou Men 4
三个贵州人

The Tree 5
树

Jianguomen Area **Dining**

China Grill 6
北京烤

Hatsune 7
隐泉餐厅

Lan 4
兰会所

Le Galerie 2
中国怡园

Mare 3
古老海

South Silk Road 8
茶马古道

Taj Pavillion 5
泰姬楼印度餐厅

Xiao Wang Fu 1
小王府

The Best Dining

Beijing **Dining**

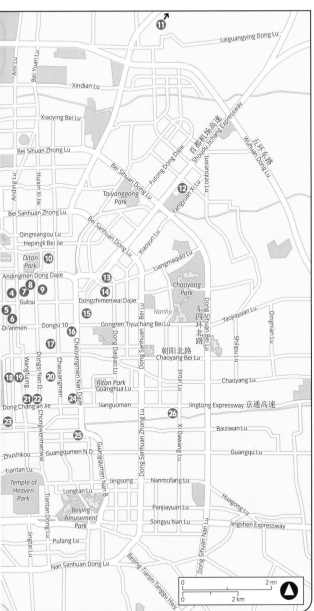

Beijing Restaurants **A to Z**

A towering dessert at Bellagio.

★ **Bei** CHAOYANG *NORTHERN ASIAN* Come here for the fantastic sushi, particularly the melt-in-your-mouth scallops and tuna tasting plate. The Korean and Chinese dishes on the menu are hit-or-miss. Bei is located in the trendy Opposite House hotel, and you can follow up dinner with a drink at one of the hotel's hip bars or a stroll around

Bei at the Opposite House hotel.

the new Sanlitun Village shopping mall (see p 66). *11 Bei Sanlitun Lu.* ☎ *010/6410-5230. ¥300–¥600. AE, DISC, MC, V. Lunch & dinner daily. Metro: Gongtibeilu. Map p 72.*

★ **Bellagio** CHAOYANG *TAIWANESE* Hip club goers frequent this Chinese version of a late-night diner for Taiwanese comfort food and spectacular ice-shaved desserts that resemble colorful mountains. *6 Gongti Xilu, south of the Gongti 100 Bowling Alley.* ☎ *010/6551-3533. ¥60–¥120. AE, DISC, MC, V. Lunch & dinner daily (open 'til 4:30am). Metro: Dongsishitiao. Map p 72.*

★ **Black Sesame Kitchen** DONGCHENG *CHINESE* Full disclosure: The author of this guide owns this restaurant and cooking school, but all the same, we vouch for it— it's one of the most unique dining experiences in town. The kitchen hosts a community dinner on Friday nights and it's open for private bookings other days of the week. Dinner includes a 10-course meal, generous pours of imported wine, and an up-front view of the cooking. Cooking classes are offered on Thursday and Saturday or by private appointment. Reservations are a must, as the kitchen doesn't take walk-ins. *3 Heizhima Hutong (call for exact directions).* ☎ *0/136-9147-4408. ¥300–¥500. No credit cards. Reservations required. Dinner daily. Metro: Beixinqiao. Map p 74.*

★ **Capital M** DONGCHENG *CONTINENTAL* This glamorous restaurant boasts a front-and-center view of Tian'anmen Square that is unique in all of Beijing. It's perfect for a leisurely dinner or weekend brunch, with a wide range of Continental dishes on the menu, cooked by an Australian chef. Leave room for

A cooking class in progress at Black Sesame Kitchen.

dessert: The pavlova, an Australian meringue, is legendary among expat circles. *2 Qianmen Buxing Jie.* ☎ *010/6702-2727. ¥300–¥600. MC, V. Lunch & dinner daily. Metro: Qianmen. Map p 74.*

★★ **Cepe** XICHENG *ITALIAN* If you're looking to splurge on a good Western meal, do it here. Everything is outstanding at this stylish restaurant in the Ritz-Carlton, from the mushroom and cheese tart appetizer to the lobster spaghetti to the roasted veal. We love the chocolate molten cake and the tiramisu. *1 Jinchengfang Dong Jie.* ☎ *010/6601-6666. www.marriott.com. ¥400–¥600. AE, MC, V. Lunch & dinner daily. Map p 74.*

★ **China Grill** CHAOYANG *International* Located on the 66th floor of the Park Hyatt, this restaurant has vertigo-inducing views of Beijing's city lights. The menu features pricey steak and seafood, and an extensive wine list, making it a great destination for a celebratory meal. *2 Jianguomen Wai Dajie.* ☎ *010/8567-1234. ¥500–¥1,000. AE, MC, V. Lunch & dinner daily. Metro: Guomao. Map p 73.*

★ **The Courtyard** DONGCHENG *FUSION* The cozy second-floor alcove is one of our favorite spots in the city for a predinner drink. The fusion food is solid, if slightly pricey,

but you're dining in one of Beijing's finest settings—just east of the Forbidden City, with a view of the moat. *95 Donghua Men Dajie.* ☎ *010/6526-8883. Reservations recommended. ¥250–¥400. AE, DISC, MC, V. Dinner daily. Metro: Tian'anmen East. Map p 74.*

★ **Crescent Moon Muslim Restaurant** DONGCHENG XINJIANG/ MUSLIM This lively neighborhood restaurant serves dishes from China's northwest province, where Central Asian and Chinese culture have combined to produce a unique, lamb-heavy cuisine. The lamb skewers—a ubiquitous street snack in Beijing—are the best in the city. Be sure to get the chao mian pian, stir-fried noodles resembling macaroni. *16 Dongsi Liutiao.* ☎ *010/6400-5281. ¥50. No credit cards. Lunch & dinner daily. Metro: Dongsi. Map p 74.*

★ **Da Dong** DONGCHENG *PEKING DUCK* Da Dong's serves the best Peking duck in the city, edging out our former favorite, Made in China, which has slipped in recent years. The restaurant also serves a nice range of accompanying Pan-Chinese dishes in a stylish dining room. Arrive early, as they don't take reservations. *22 Dongsi Shi Tiao.* ☎ *010/5169-0329. ¥100–¥200. AE, DISC, MC, V. Lunch & dinner daily. Metro: Dongsishitiao. Map p 74.*

Capital M's breathtaking view of Tian'anmen Square.

★ **Dali Courtyard** DONGCHENG *YUNNAN* Romance, romance! Old jazz tunes play in a traditional Chinese courtyard decorated with coal furnaces and Art Deco furniture. There's no menu—the chef serves up a set meal in courses—so it's perfect for couples or small groups who want to try a range of southwestern Chinese dishes. *67 Xiaojingchang Hutong, Gulou Dongdajie.* ☎ *010/ 8404-1430. ¥100–¥300 set dinner, ¥100–¥300 lunch. AE, MC, V. Lunch & dinner daily. Metro: Beixinqiao. Map p 74.*

★★ kids **Din Tai Fung** CHAOYANG *SHANGHAINESE* This popular Taiwanese-owned restaurant with locations around Asia is the only place in Beijing where you'll find good xiao long bao, or Shanghai-style soup dumplings. The second floor features a kids' playroom. *24 Xinyuanli Zhong Jie.* ☎ *010/6462-4502. ¥100–¥200. AE, DISC, MC, V.*

Lunch & dinner daily. Metro: Nongzhanguan. Map p 74.

★ **Ding Ding Xiang** DONGCHENG *CHINESE HOTPOT* This stylish restaurant frequented by Chinese celebrities is where we go when we're in the mood for Chinese fondue, a dish that's too often served in grimy, cheap restaurants. Diners cook fresh veggies and quality meats in small individual pots at the table. Arrive early or be prepared to wait. *2/F, Yuanjia International Apartments, Dongzhimenwai, Dongzhong Jie (opposite East Gate Plaza).* ☎ *010/6417-9289. ¥100–¥150. DISC, MC, V. Lunch & dinner daily. Metro: Dongzhimen. Map p 74.*

★ **Element Fresh** CHAOYANG *AMERICAN* If you're looking for healthy salads, smoothies, and light Continental dishes, this restaurant is the place to go. Located in the Sanlitun Village mall, this restaurant offers a stylish interior and a nice outdoor patio for Beijing's warmer months. Weekend brunches here are popular with expats. *19 Sanlitun Lu.* ☎ *010/ 6417-1318. ¥100–¥200. AE, DISC, MC, V. Lunch & dinner daily. Metro: Gongtibeilu. Map p 72.*

Diners cook their own meats and veggies fondue-style at Ding Ding Xiang.

Feiteng Yuxiang CHAOYANG *SICH-UANESE* If you wish, you can see the live fish you selected for your meal hacked into pieces. The shuizhu yu, or water-cooked fish, is a misnomer for the restaurant's most popular dish. The fish is actually cooked mostly in oil with mouth-burning spices—but it's still delicious. *1 Gongti Beilu.* ☎ *010/6417-4988. ¥50–¥80. No credit cards. Lunch & dinner daily. Metro: Dongsishitiao. Map p 72.*

Green T. House CHAOYANG *FUSION* This overrated yet popular place is not a teahouse, but a restaurant that serves über-pretentious, mediocre meals. You may hear raves about it from out- of-towners who have enjoyed the exclusive feel, the exaggerated decor, and the copious amounts of dry ice used in the presentation of dishes. *6 Gongti Xilu.* ☎ *010/6552-8310. ¥200–¥400. AE, DISC, MC, V. Lunch & dinner daily. Metro: Dongsishitiao. Map p 72.*

★ **Han Cang** XICHENG *HAKKA* The lovely lakeside views, comfortable tables, and delicious dishes—like the paper-wrapped fish and shrimp skewers—make this restaurant one of our favorite places to take out-of-town visitors. *12 Qianhai Nan Yan.* ☎ *010/6404-2259. ¥50–¥100. No credit cards. Lunch &*

dinner daily. Metro: Zhangzizhonglu. Map p 71.

★ **Hatsune** CHAOYANG *JAPANESE* Japanese food is widely available in Beijing, but this is our favorite place to get the popular American versions of Japanese cooking, with favorites such as California and spider rolls. Paying homage to the capital, the restaurant also features a Beijing duck roll with duck, hoisin sauce, and cucumbers. *2/F Heqiao Bldg. C, 8 Guanghua Donglu Jia.* ☎ *010/6581-3939. ¥150–¥250. AE, DISC, MC, V. Lunch & dinner daily. Metro: Guomao. Map p 73.*

Huajia Yiyuan DONGCHENG *CHINESE* Located in a sprawling outdoor courtyard, this bargain restaurant is one of the few that we'll visit on the popular dining street called Gui Jie (Ghost St.). Unlike many of the other restaurants on this street, Huajia Yiyuan serves a wide range of good-quality Chinese dishes, including a decent Peking duck. *235 Dongzhimen Nei Dajie.* ☎ *010/6403-0677. ¥40–¥60. AE, DISC, MC, V. Open 24 hr. Metro: Beixinqiao. Map p 74.*

Hutong Pizza DONGCHENG *PIZZA* We call this place for delivery whenever a pie craving strikes. The restaurant itself is worth a trip—located down a small alley and decorated

Preparing Peking duck at Dadong.

The glossy setting at Green T. House is part of the appeal.

with a pond and Chinese furniture, it's an unlikely but refreshing atmosphere in which to enjoy gigantic slices with a huge selection of toppings. *9 Yinding Qiao Hutong.* ☎ *010/8322-8916. ¥60–¥100. No credit cards. Lunch & dinner daily. Metro: Gulou. Map p 71.*

★ **Karaiya Spice House** CHAOYANG *HUNAN* A sister restaurant of Hatsune, this trendy restaurant owned by a Chinese-American entrepreneur makes spicy Hunan cuisine accessible for an international audience. The hot-and-sour pork ribs and the Mandarin fish with red and yellow chilies are signature items. *Sanlitun Village, 3rd floor, Sanlitun Bei Lu.* ☎ *010/6415-3535. ¥100–¥200. AE, MC, V. Lunch & dinner daily. Metro: Gongtibeilu. Map p 72.*

Kong Yi Ji DONGCHENG *SHANGHAINESE* This restaurant by Houhai Lake is one of the city's few places to get solid Shanghainese fare. It's named after a drunken scholar in a novel by Lu Xun, one of China's most famous authors. Especially good is the dongpo rou, sugar and soy-sauce-infused slices of fatty pork, and crystal river shrimp. *Deshengmen Nei Da Jie.* ☎ *010/6618-4917. ¥80–¥120. AE, MC, DC, V. Lunch & dinner daily. Metro: Jishuitan. Map p 71.*

Lan CHAOYANG *SICHUANESE/ FUSION* European Renaissance–style paintings hang on the wall, and cabinets hold wacky items such as stacks of canned tuna and Mao memorabilia. Designed by Philippe Starck, this flagship of a popular chain of Sichuan restaurants serves decent, if overpriced, dishes. Avoid the fusion fare at all costs, and stick to basics such as the kungpao chicken. *4th Floor, LG Twins Tower, 12 Jianguomenwai Dajie Yi.* ☎ *010/5109-6012. ¥200–¥400. AE, DISC, MC, V. Lunch & dinner daily. Metro: Yonganli. Map p 73.*

★ **Le Galerie** CHAOYANG *DIM SUM/CANTONESE* There's a debate among certain expat circles as to whether this restaurant, or Lei Garden, is the best dim sum restaurant in town. The prices here are lower and the traditional courtyard setting might tip the scale in Le Galerie's direction. On the southern edge of Ritan Park, you can stroll through the nice grounds to work off the calories. *Ritan Park South Gate.* ☎ *010/8562-8698. ¥100–¥150. AE, DISC, MC, V. Lunch & dinner daily. Metro: Jianguomen. Map p 73.*

★ **Lei Garden** DONGCHENG *DIM SUM/CANTONESE* This branch of a popular Hong Kong restaurant serves a great selection of classic dim sum items. There's always a buzz here, whether it's filled with power lunchers on the weekdays or wealthy families on the weekends. If you're looking for something a little more relaxed, head to Le Galerie. *89 Jinbao Jie.* ☎ *010/8522-1212. ¥150– ¥250. AE, DISC, MC, V. Lunch & dinner daily. Metro: Dengshikou. Map p 74.*

Li Jia Cai DONGCHENG (XICHENG) *IMPERIAL CHINESE* Even though we're not huge fans of imperial cuisine—the food supposedly served to Qing dynasty royalty—we make an exception for this restaurant, hidden in the hutongs. The set-menu meals are priced between ¥200 and ¥2,000 per person, so a trip here can fit any visitor's budget. *11 Yangfang Hutong. Deshengmen Nei Dajie.* ☎ *010/6618-0107. ¥200–¥2,000. No credit cards. Dinner daily. Metro: Gulou. Map p 71.*

★ **Luce** XICHENG *ITALIAN* This is our favorite neighborhood Italian restaurant; it has a cool, minimalist feel rather than red-checked tablecloths. We especially love the penne with Chinese truffles and the lamb chops. *138 Jiugulou Dajie.* ☎ *010/ 8402-4417. ¥100–¥200. No credit cards. Lunch & dinner daily. Metro: Gulou. Map p 71.*

★ **Made in China** DONGCHENG *NORTHERN CHINESE* The openkitchen setting, where you can see chefs wok-frying and wrapping dumplings, lets you in on the action. In recent years, quality has slipped here, but it still remains a perennial favorite for Peking duck and inventive ice cream flavors such as jasmine tea and champagne pear made on the premises. Expect to pay higher prices than for your usual Chinese meal, but some think that the buzzy ambience is worth it. *1/F Grand Hyatt Hotel, 1 Dongchang'an Jie.* ☎ *010/6510-9608. ¥250–¥500. AE, DISC, MC, V. Lunch & dinner daily. Metro: Wangfujing. Map p 74.*

★ **Maison Boulud** CHAOYANG *FRENCH* Ever since New York celebrity chef Daniel Boulud opened his first outpost in Asia, there's been little reason to go anywhere else in Beijing for French food. Housed in the former (pre-1949) American embassy, Boulud's refined "soul" food gleams brilliantly. The prices here, while still high, are cheaper than what they'd be in New York. *23 Qianmen Dong Da Jie.* ☎ *010/6559-9200. ¥500–¥1,000. AE, DISC, MC, V. Lunch & dinner daily. Metro: Qianmen. Map p 74.*

★★ **Mare** CHAOYANG *SPANISH* The huge range of tapas, the large wine list, and the elegant, comfortable dining room make us regulars at this restaurant. We love the mushroom risotto and the deep-fried baby squid. The chocolate molten cake, flanked with small scoops of hazelnut and vanilla ice cream, is our favorite dessert in town. *12 Guanghua Lu.* ☎ *010/6595-4178. ¥200–¥300. AE, MC, V. Lunch & dinner daily. Metro: Guomao. Map p 73.*

★ **Mosto** CHAOYANG *CONTEMPORARY SOUTH AMERICAN* With an urban-hip feel, this restaurant serves inventive flavors, created by a South American chef, that include ceviches and steaks. A good-value wine list rounds out a pleasant dining experience. The set lunches, at ¥70, are a

The entrance to Le Galerie.

Prepping meals at Made in China.

good value. *Nali Patio, 81 Sanlitun Bei Lu.* ☎ *010/5208-6030. ¥200–¥400. AE, MC, V. Lunch & dinner daily. Metro: Gongtibeilu. Map p 72.*

My Humble House DONGCHENG *MODERN CHINESE* A good choice if you're on an expense account—you'll be in the company of plenty of business-suit types. While the food is fusion, it manages to be solid without being too pretentious. The sliced roasted duck and the roasted rack of lamb are particularly delicious. Reserve a table by the reflecting pool. *1/F, West Bldg. 3, Oriental Plaza, 1 Dong Chang'an Jie.* ☎ *010/ 8518-8811. ¥300–¥500. AE, DISC, MC, V. Lunch & dinner daily. Metro: Wangfujing. Map p 74.*

Maison Boulud.

No Name Restaurant XICHENG *YUNNAN* Hidden down a narrow alley is this little gem serving small portions of noodles, grilled meats, and stir-fries. Order an extra drink and kick back in the Mediterranean-style dining room—the service is super slow. *1 Da Jinsi Hutong.* ☎ *010/6618-6061. ¥80–¥120. AE, MC, V. Lunch & dinner daily. Metro: Gulou. Map p 71.*

★ **Noodle Loft** CHAOYANG *NORTHERN CHINESE* This popular restaurant serves more kinds of noodles than you ever knew existed. And the noodle chefs displaying their skills are nothing short of performance artists. One dish consists of a single long, hand-pulled noodle. The restaurant can arrange noodle-making classes in the afternoons; book ahead. *20 Xi Dawang Lu.* ☎ *010/6774-9950. ¥80–¥150. AE, DISC, MC, V. Lunch & dinner daily. Metro: Dawanglu. Map p 74.*

★ **Nuage** XICHENG *VIETNAMESE* Rickshaws and Chinese antiques give Nuage's dining room a rustic feel, while the roof offers a panoramic view of the Drum Tower area. We love the Vietnamese coffee and the spring rolls. *22 Qianhai Dong Yan.* ☎ *010/6401-9581. ¥150–¥250. AE, DISC, MC, V. Lunch & dinner daily. Metro: Gulou. Map p 71.*

The reflecting pool at My Humble House.

★★ **The Orchard** CHAOYANG *CONTINENTAL* This is by far our favorite place for Sunday brunch, and the 45-minute drive from central Beijing gives us a whiff of fresh country—or at least fresh suburban—air. The ¥160 buffet offers delicious salads, broiled fish, and yummy desserts. Take a stroll in the rambling organic orchard and the boutique store after you've indulged. *Hegezhuang Cun, Cuigezhuang Xiang (call before you go for detailed directions; reservations highly recommended).* ☎ *010/6433-6270. ¥150–¥250. AE, MC, V. Lunch & dinner Tues–Sun. No metro. Map p 74.*

Pure Lotus CHAOYANG *VEGETARIAN* The presentation is slightly over the top, but since decent

vegetarian fare is hard to come by in Beijing, we won't protest too much. A monk supposedly owns the restaurant, but we suspect that he's more of a businessman, given the relatively high prices. *10 Nongzhanguan Nan Lu (inside Zhongguo Wenlian).* ☎ *010/6592-3627. ¥200–¥400. AE, DISC, MC, V. Lunch & dinner daily. Metro: Nongzhanguan. Map p 74.*

★ **Shuang Fu** DONGCHENG *NORTHERN CHINESE* This inexpensive, local restaurant rarely frequented by foreigners serves simple, delicious northern dishes that are heavy on the potatoes and noodles. The mati shaobing, or biscuits shaped like horse hooves served with beef, are worth the trip alone. *9 Heping Li Wuqu, East gate*

Exotic Eating

Beijingers have fairly tame tastes in comparison to their southern Chinese counterparts. If you consider yourself an adventurous eater, you might want to visit **Wangfujing Night Market** (Wangfujing yeshi, west of Sundongan Guangchang; no phone). Among the regular skewered meats served at this night market are sticks of scorpions and silkworms and other bugs. The scorpions taste like popcorn, and the silkworms have a distinct nutty flavor—and yes, we've tasted them all. The price is ¥5 per stick, and dinner is served daily. *Map p 74.*

The loftlike dining room at South Silk Road.

of Ditan Park. ☎ 010/8422-2388. ¥30–¥50. No credit cards. Lunch & dinner daily. Metro: Yonghegong. Map p 74.

★★ **Sichuan Provincial Restaurant** DONGCHENG *SICHUANESE* Owned by the Sichuan government, this bargain restaurant serves traditional fare guaranteed to set your mouth on fire. The dining room is lively and very crowded. *5 Gongyuan Tou Tiao, Jianguomen Nei Dajie.* ☎ 010/6512-2277. ¥30–¥50. No credit cards. Lunch & dinner daily. Metro: Jianguomen. Map p 74.

Source DONGCHENG *SICHUANESE* Frequented by expats, this restaurant in a Chinese courtyard is where you should go if you want to enjoy a quiet Sichuanese meal in style. The set menu served in courses can be hit or miss. *14 Banchang Hutong, Kuanjie Nan Luogu Xiang.* ☎ 010/6400-3736. ¥150–¥200. AE, MC, V. Lunch & dinner daily. Map p 74.

South Silk Road CHAOYANG *YUNNAN* This was one of the first restaurants to serve Yunnan cuisine, quickly setting a trend. The dining room feels like a warehouse loft and is popular with locals and contemporary artists. We recommend the guoqiao mixian, or cross bridge noodles. *3/F Bldg. D, SOHO Xiandai Cheng, 88 Juanguo Lu.* ☎ 010/8580-4286.

¥80–¥120. AE, DISC, MC, V. Lunch & dinner daily. Metro: Dawanglu. Map p 73.

★ **Sureño** CHAOYANG *MEDITTERANEAN* The menu isn't particularly flashy—pastas, pizzas, and grilled meats dominate—yet the classy atmosphere and service make it almost a fine-dining experience. Located in the Opposite House hotel, the restaurant puts you right in the heart of Beijing's nightlife scene, with two hip bars in the hotel and many others in the vicinity. *11 Sanlitun Bei Lu.* ☎ 010/6410-5240. ¥250–¥400. AE, DISC, MC, V. Lunch & dinner daily. Metro: Gongtibeilu. Map p 72.

Taj Pavilion CHAOYANG *INDIAN* The Indian community in Beijing generally agrees that the Taj serves the city's best Indian food. Though a bit pricey, it's the best place to take care of your saag paneer or chicken tikka craving. *L1-28 West Wing of China World Trade Center, 1 Jianguo Men Wai Dajie.* ☎ 010/6505-5866. ¥250–¥350. AE, DISC, MC, V. Lunch & dinner daily. Metro: Gulou. Map p 73.

★ **Three Guizhou Men** CHAOYANG *GUIZHOU* Sour and spicy, the Guizhou cuisine here is popular with hip and trendy Chinese. Though we like the popular hot pot, we never fail to order the cuigu (ribs) and tudou ni (mashed potatoes). *2/F, Bldg. 8,*

Gongti Xi Lu. ☎ 010/6551-8517. ¥80–¥120. AE, MC, V. Open 24 hr. Metro: Dongsishitiao. Map p 72.

★ **The Tree** CHAOYANG PIZZA Wash down the Tree's excellent thin-crust pizza with one of their many beers. Expats gather here nearly every night of the week. *Nan 43 Sanlitun Bei Jie.* ☎ 010/6415-1954. ¥80–¥120. No credit cards. Lunch & dinner daily. Metro: Gongti-beilu. Map p 72.

★ **Vineyard Café** DONGCHENG CONTINENTAL This is one of our favorite new neighborhood haunts—the sunny outdoor patio is a great place to enjoy lunch or Sunday brunch. The cafe also boasts wireless Internet access and a good wine selection. *31 Wudaoying Hutong (just north of the Confucius Temple).* ☎ 010/6402-7961. ¥50–¥150. MC, V. Lunch & dinner Tues–Sun (closed Mon). Metro: Yonghegong. Map p 74.

★ **Xian'r Lao Man** DONGCHENG BEIJING Beijing cuisine isn't exactly a regional highlight of Chinese cuisine—except when it comes to dumplings. Happily, inexpensive Xian'r Lao Man has 60 kinds of fillings to choose from. We love the cabbage and peanut, and the pork and corn dumplings so much that I once interned in the kitchen to learn how to wrap them myself. *252 Andingmen Nei Dajie.* ☎ 010/6404-6944. ¥20–¥40. No credit cards. Lunch & dinner daily. Metro: Andingmen. Map p 74.

★ **Xiao Wang Fu** CHAOYANG CHINESE So far, this is the only place we know of in Beijing where you can get lemon chicken. (Don't be embarrassed to order a serving.) The restaurant also serves a very solid Peking duck and xiangla jidjing, deep-fried chicken with loads of red peppers. The rooftop deck is enjoyable in the warmer months. *North Gate of Ritan Park, Ritan Bei Lu.* ☎ 010/8561-5985. ¥80–¥150. AE, DISC, MC, V. Lunch & dinner daily. Metro: Guanghualu. Map p 73.

★ **Xinjiang Islam Restaurant** XICHENG XINJIANG/MUSLIM Eating at this restaurant feels like a visit to Central Asia. Groups of men with moustaches and fur caps tuck into a meal of chewy noodles and lamb skewers in the giant mess hall. This place is as good for people-watching as it is for the food. We recommend the kao yangrou baozi (buns filled with lamb). *7 Sanlihe Lu, Xinjiang Provincial Government Office.*

Enjoying a meal on Vineyard's sunny patio.

The rooftop deck at Xiao Wang Fu.

☎ 010/6833-5599. ¥30–¥60. No credit cards. Lunch & dinner daily. Metro: Dongsi. Map p 74.

★ **Yotsuba** CHAOYANG *JAPANESE* A Japanese chef works in front of a small bar, where you can sit and watch the action. It's a tiny place, consisting of the bar and three tables, and the exclusive experience is not to be missed if you are a sushi fan. Be sure to book several days in advance. *2 Xinyuanli Zhong Jie.* ☎ 010/6467-1837. ¥250–¥500. AE, DISC, MC, V. Dinner only Tues–Sun. Metro: Nongzhanguan. Map p 74.

Yue Lu DONGCHENG *HUNAN* Spicy Hunan cuisine is served in a lakeside setting decorated with traditional Chinese furniture. The duojiao yutou (fish head with chili peppers) is highly recommended. *51-10 Di'anmen Xi Dajie.* ☎ 010/6617-2696. ¥80–¥120. No credit cards. Lunch & dinner daily. Metro: Zhangzizhonglu. Map p 71.

★ **Yunteng Binguan** DONGCHENG (CHONGWEN) *YUNNAN* There's no atmosphere to speak of, but this is the place to try authentic Yunnan cuisine. Specialties include mushrooms and other fungus, grilled cheese, and chicken simmered in a pot. *Yunnan*

Provincial Government Office, 7 Donghuashi Beili Dongqu. ☎ 010/6713-6439. ¥40–¥80. No credit cards. Lunch & dinner daily. Metro: Jianguomen. Map p 74.* ●

Patrons dine on authentic Yunnan cuisine at Yunteng.

Nightlife **Best Bets**

Best **Gay Club**
★ Destination, *7 Gongti Xilu (p 100)*

Best for **Wine & Cheese**
★★ Scarlett, *Hotel G, A7 Gongti Xilu (p 102)*

Best **Martini**
★★ Q Bar, *6/F of Eastern Inn Hotel (p 97)*

Best **Karaoke**
Karaoke Partyworld, *1/F Fanli Bldg., 22 Chaowai Dajie (p 100)*

Best **Hotel Bar**
Punk, *The Opposite House, 11 Sanlitun Bei Lu (p 98)*

Best **Find in a Hutong**
★ Bed, *17 Zhangwang Hutong (p 94)*

Best for **Chinese Celebrity Spotting**
Lan, *4F LG Twin Towers, 12B Jianguomenwai Dajie (p 95)*

Best **Open-Air Bar**
★ Face Bar, *26 Dongcaoyuan, Gongti Nan Lu (p 95)*; and Xiu, *Park Hyatt, 2 Jianguomenwai Da Jie (p 97)*

Best **'80s Night**
★ Alfa, *5 Xingfu Yicun (p 94)*

Best for **Live Experimental Music**
MAO Livehouse, *111 Gulou Da Jie (p 101)*; and Yugong Yushan, *3-2 Zhangzhizhong Lu (p 101)*

Best **Foreign Exchange Student Meat Market**
Propaganda, *100m (328 ft.) north of the east gate of Huaqing Jiayuan (p 98)*

Best **Pub**
Black Sun Bar, *Chaoyang Park West Gate (p 102)*

Best **Open-Mic Nights**
Lush, *2/F, 1 Huaqing Jiayuan (p 95)*

Best **Sports Bar**
The Pavillion, *8 Gongtixi Lu (p 96)*

Best **Bar for Homesick Americans**
Blue Frog, *3F-S4 Tower, Sanlitun Village (p 94)*

Best for **Late-Night Chats**
Apothecary, *3/F-Nali Patio, 81 Sanlitun Beilu (p 94)*

Belting it out at Karaoke Partyworld. Previous page: A rave in a Beijing bar.

Houhai Lake Area Nightlife

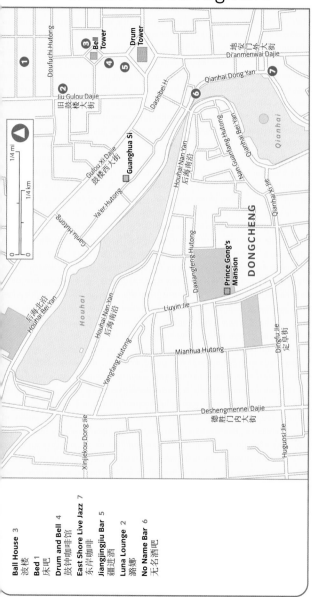

Ball House 3
波楼

Bed 1
床吧

Drum and Bell 4
鼓钟咖啡馆

East Shore Live Jazz 7
东岸咖啡

Jiangjingjiu Bar 5
疆进酒

Luna Lounge 2
潞娜

No Name Bar 6
无名酒吧

Sanlitun Nightlife

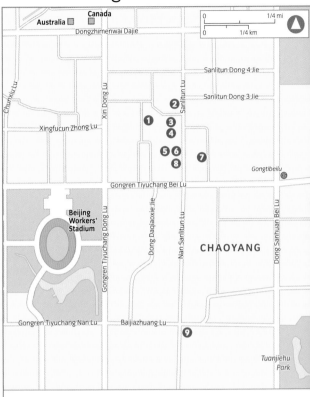

Australia
Canada
Dongzhimenwai Dajie
Chunxiu Lu
Sanlitun Dong 4 Jie
Xin Dong Lu
Sanlitun Dong 3 Jie
Sanlitun Lu
❷
Xingfucun Zhong Lu
❶
❸
❹
❺ ❻
❼
❽
Gongtibeilu
Gongren Tiyuchang Bei Lu
Beijing
Workers'
Stadium
Gongren Tiyuchang Dong Lu
Dong Daqiaoxie Jie
Nan Sanlitun Lu
CHAOYANG
Dong Sanhuan Bei Lu
Gongren Tiyuchang Nan Lu
Baijiazhuang Lu
❾
Tuanjiehu
Park

Apothecary 6

Bar Blu 4
蓝吧

Blue Frog 8
蓝娃

Jazz-Ya 7
爵士

Punk 2

Q-Bar 9
麦芽咖啡厅

Saddle 5

The Tree 1
树

White Rabbit 3

Summer Palace

BEIJING

Chaoyang Park

Forbidden City

Tian'anmen Sq.

Map Area

Temple of
Heaven

Workers' Stadium Nightlife

Alfa 2
阿尔法

Coco Banana 6
芭娜娜酒吧

Destination 8
目的地

Face Bar 9
妃思

Mix 3
密克斯

The Pavillion 5
万龙腾飞

Scarlett 7

Red Ball 1
足球俱乐部和酒吧

Vic's 4
威克斯

Beijing Nightlife

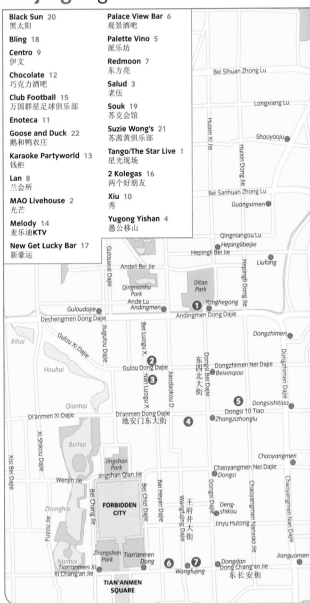

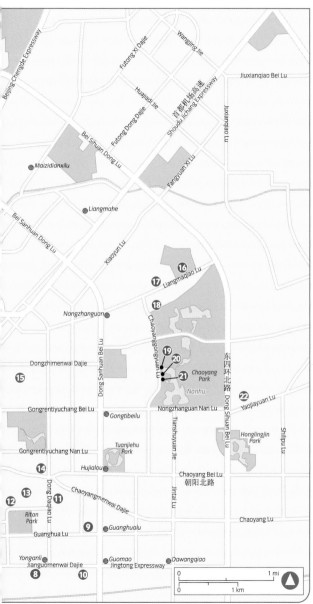

University District Nightlife

Summer Palace
Map Area
BEIJING
Chaoyang Park
Forbidden City
Tian'anmen Sq.
Temple of Heaven

TSINGHUA UNIVERSITY

Shuangqing Lu

Wudaokou

Chengfu Lu

中关村北大街 Zhongguancun Bei Dajie

HAIDIAN

PEKING UNIVERSITY

Zhongguancun Dong Lu

Caijing Dong Lu

❶

❷
❸
❹

Bei Shiuan Xi Lu
北四环路

Kexueyuan Nan Lu

D-22	1
Lush	2
Propaganda	4
Zub	3

0 — 500 ft
0 — 100 m

Beijing Nightlife A to Z

Bars

★ **Alfa** CHAOYANG   This Southeast Asian bar features comfy private booths on the second floor and an outdoor patio. The small, claustrophobic dance floor is fun on Fridays when the DJ spins '80s music. *5 Xingfu Yicun (in the alley opposite the Workers' Stadium).* ☎ *010/6413-0086. Metro: Dongsishitiao. Map p 91.*

★★ **Apothecary** CHAOYANG Featuring drinks from America's South such as mint juleps, whiskeys, and bourbons, this wood-paneled wall bar has become a favorite among Beijing's expat community. The bar is partly owned by an American chef with southern roots, and

he's cooked up a nice side menu of dishes to go along with the drinks. *3/F-Nali Patio, 81 Sanlitun Beilu.* ☎ *010/5208-6040. Metro: Gongtibeilu. Map p 90.*

★★ **Bed** XICHENG   On Saturday nights, you're most likely to find us here—we love the mojitos and sangrias and the bar's minimalist yet traditional Chinese feel. The DJ spins techno and house, while locals lounge in the outdoor courtyard and smaller alcoves furnished with opium beds. *17 Zhangwang Hutong.* ☎ *010/8400-1554. Metro: Gulou. Map p 89.*

★ **Blue Frog** CHAOYANG   If you're craving a taste of America, head to this bar and restaurant

Apothecary.

featuring a good selection of beers and wines and casual dining—in the warmer months, you'll find a nice alfresco patio to soak up the sun, plus it's centrally located in the Sanlitun Village mall (p 66). *3F-S4 Tower, Village at Sanlitun.* ☎ *010/6417-4030. Metro: Gongtibeilu. Map p 90.*

Drum and Bell DONGCHENG We love the intimate atmosphere of this place, nestled between the Drum and Bell towers. The rooftop patio overlooks a courtyard where you often see locals playing Chinese hacky sack or a casual game of soccer. Stoves inside keep Drum and Bell toasty warm in the winter. *41 Zhonglouwan Hutong.* ☎ *010/8403-3600. Metro: Gulou. Map p 89.*

★ **Face Bar** CHAOYANG Penny-pinching Beijing expats complain about the exorbitant prices for drinks at Face Bar, but it's still cheaper than Hong Kong or New York. Plus, you get a sophisticated, Southeast Asian–inspired decor that incorporates Buddhist statues. The bar also contains the restaurant

Hazara. *26 Dongcaoyuan, Gongti Nan Lu (just south of Workers' Stadium south gate).* ☎ *010/6551-6788. Metro: Chaoyangmen. Map p 91.*

Jazz-Ya CHAOYANG We've had more than one nasty hangover from drinking pitchers of Long Island iced teas at this place. But still we go back—we can't help ourselves—they're the best drinks in town. This bar is a great place to have loud, inebriated chats with 20 of your closest friends. *18 Sanlitun Beilu (beside Nali Market).* ☎ *010/6415-1227. Metro: Gongtibeilu. Map p 90.*

Lan CHAOYANG European paintings hang on the ceiling, while the cabinets contain random collections of books, pickles, and cans of tuna. It's a bad Philippe Starck nightmare, yet somehow a hit among Beijing's expats and nouveau riche. *4F LG Twin Towers, 12B Jianguomenwai Dajie.* ☎ *010/5109-6012. Metro: Jianguomen. Map p 92.*

Luna Lounge DONGCHENG This is a perfect place to host a small party. The lounge is beautifully designed and decorated. It's part of the restaurant Luce, so if you fancy a plate of truffle penne with that glass of white wine, you're in the right place. *138 Jiu Gulou Dajie.* ☎ *010/8402-4417. Metro: Gulou. Map p 89.*

★ **Lush** HAIDIAN This modest bar has everything a student could ask for—great live music and cheap drinks. Lush has regular open mic nights, movie nights, and weekend DJ sets. *2/F, 1 Huaqing Jiayuan.* ☎ *010/8286-3566. www.lushbeijing. com. ¥10–¥20 cover. Metro: Wuda-okou. Map p 94.*

★ **No Name Bar** XICHENG We're longtime loyal customers of this bar, the first to open at Houhai Lake in

A view of the popular Houhai Lake bar and restaurant area.

2000. Dozens of copycats now dot the grounds around the lake, but none have been able to duplicate No Name's terrific formula of relaxed, chill-out vibe and simple cocktails. *3 Qianhai Dongyan.* ☎ *010/6401-8541. Metro: Gulou. Map p 89.*

Palace View Bar DONGCHENG Come for the view, the best panorama in Beijing, which more than makes up for the mediocre drinks. Open June to October. *35 Dong Chang'an Jie.* ☎ *010/6513-7788, ext. 458. Metro: Tian'anmen East. Map p 92.*

The Pavillion CHAOYANG Nestled in a park, this place is a refuge from some of Beijing's loudest and most obnoxious nightclubs. The Pavillion has a sophisticated European decor and possibly the largest, grassiest outdoor seating area the city has to offer. For major sporting events, they set up a giant outdoor screen in the huge backyard, making it the perfect place to kick back with some friends and a beer. *8 Gongtixi Lu (opposite west gate of Workers' Stadium).* ☎ *010/6507-2617. Metro: Dongsishitiao. Map p 91.*

Salud DONGCHENG Most of the bars on Nanluoguxiang are boring places with bad music and really bad drinks. Salud is an exception. The cozy chairs make it a perfect place to chill out with a group of friends, and the drinks are made with attention to detail. *66 Nanluoguxiang.* ☎ *010/6402-5086. Metro: Beixiniqao. Map p 92.*

Souk Lounge CHAOYANG Souk is kind of like Bed (p 94), but for people who live on the east side of town. They have antique opium beds where you can cozy up with friends over drinks and an order of strawberry-flavored tobacco served in a water bong. *West Gate of Chaoyang Park (in the alley next to Italian restaurant Annie's).* ☎ *010/6506-7309. Map p 92.*

Cocktail Bars
★ **Centro** CHAOYANG It's been a standby for more than a decade, and continues to be popular among the business suits, but Centro's feeling a little worn these days. It's a decent place for a cocktail if you happen to be in the area, though,

and occasional jazz nights liven up the scene. *1/F Kerry Centre Hotel, 1 Guanghua Lu.* ☎ *010/6561-8833, ext. 42. Metro: Guomao. Map p 92.*

★★ **Q Bar** CHAOYANG Technically, it's a hotel bar, but Q is a couple of steps up from its bland two-star surroundings. The bartenders, George and Echo, are legendary for mixing the city's best cocktails, and the rooftop deck attracts a solid following of expats. *6/F of Eastern Inn Hotel (intersection of Sanlitun Nan Lu and Gongti Nan Lu).* ☎ *010/6595-9239. www. qbarbeijing.com. Map p 90.*

Redmoon DONGCHENG Somewhat stuffy and full of Rolex-sporting businessmen, this bar in the Grand Hyatt serves excellent mixed sake drinks (try the mojito sake) and has a sushi bar. *1 Dong Chang'an Dajie (main floor of Grand Hyatt Hotel).* ☎ *010/8518-1234, ext. 6366. Metro: Wangfujing. Map p 92.*

The Saddle CHAOYANG This popular Mexican cantina serves the usual drinks you'd expect to find in such a setting (margaritas, daiquiris, beers) and decent bar food. Located in the Sanlitun bar area, there are plenty of places a hop away from here. *2/F-Nali Patio East, 81 Sanlitun Beilu.* ☎ *010/5208-6005. Metro: Tuanjiehu. Map p 90.*

The Tree CHAOYANG The Tree has a great selection of beers (we're addicted to the Belgian framboise), plus good thin-crust pizza. A cover band usually plays on weekends. *43 Sanlitun Beijie (behind Poacher's Inn).* ☎ *010/6415-1954. Metro: Gongtibeilu. Map p 90.*

★ **Xiu** CHAOYANG One of the more flashier settings to hit Beijing in the last year or so, Xiu delivers a happening scene, cocktails, and a nice outdoor patio for the warmer months. It's the perfect place for impressing

someone, as it's part of the glittering new Park Hyatt hotel, one of the most prestigious addresses in town. *F/6-Park Hyatt Beijing, 2 Jianguomenwai Da Jie.* ☎ *010/85671108. Metro: Guomao. Map p 92.*

Dance Clubs

Cover Charges

Beijing clubs usually don't have a cover charge. Visiting international DJs or live music acts are the exceptions, but rarely will you pay more than ¥50.

Bar Blu CHAOYANG They love to spin Top 40 tunes, and it can be a bit of a meat market on the weekends, but it's all in good fun. Weekday happy hours are downright dangerous. Servers bring you a remote control, you press a button, and depending on your luck you might get a two-for-one deal, pay ¥20 for anything, or get drinks on the house. We're usually shattered by six. *4/F, 5/F Tongli Studio, Sanlitun Bei Jie.* ☎ *010/6417-4124. Metro: Tuanjiehu. Map p 90.*

★ **Bling** CHAOYANG The name explains it all. This club prides itself on being glamorous and indulgent, from the half Cadillac DJ booth whose various DJs play dance and hip-hop music, to the "diamond" shades that section off the rooms. The crowd generally gets glammed up to party and orders bottles of liquor or champagne for a potentially rowdy night. *Solana #5–1, 6 Chaoyang Park Rd.* ☎ *010/5905-6999. Metro: Map p 92.*

★ **Chocolate** CHAOYANG Frequented by vodka-shooting Central Asians and Russians, this nightclub is a one-of-a-kind experience if you're up for an adventure. *19 Ritan Beilu (northwest corner of Ritan*

A night view of the Sanlitun scene.

Park). ☎ 010/8561-3988. www.club-chocolate.ru. Map p 92.

Coco Banana CHAOYANG   One of the newest nightclubs on the scene, this venue hosts big international DJs. They draw a good dancing crowd with their hip floor and live go-go dancers.*6 Gongti Xilu.* ☎ 010/8599-9999. www.ve-v.com. Metro: Dongsishitiao. Map p 91.

Mix CHAOYANG   Truth be told, the muscle-bound bouncers at this club scare us. But all that muscle is in place to keep out the riffraff and make sure nothing but good, clean fun is taking place inside this thumping hip-hop/DJ-beats nightclub. *Inside North Gate of Workers' Stadium.* ☎ 010/6530-2889. Metro: Dongsishitiao. Map p 91.

New Get Lucky Bar CHAOYANG   A large dance floor full of young things gyrating to hip-hop beats make your chances of getting lucky pretty decent. *A1 Xingba Lu, Nuren Jie.* ☎ 010/8448-3335. Map p 92.

Propaganda HAIDIAN   This is the place to see (and hope that you're

not seen). Propaganda is the bass pumping club of the student district. Its dance floor has witnessed many a hot and heavy make-out session. *100m (328 ft.) north of the east gate of Huaqing Jiayuan.* ☎ 010/8289-3991. Metro: Wudaokou. Map p 94.

★★ **Punk** CHAOYANG   Located in the Opposite House hotel, this basement club hosts many local and foreign DJs and offers an innovative drink list. Its intimate size makes it more approachable for those wary of stadium-size dance halls. **Mesh,** a more sedate lounge one floor above Punk, caters to a gay- friendly crowd and serves delicious cocktails like the passion fruit and lychee martinis. *B/1-The Opposite House, 11 Sanlitun Bei Lu.* ☎ 010/6410-5222. www.barpunk.com. Metro: Tuanjiehu. Map p 90.

Suzie Wong's CHAOYANG   Suzie's attracts a mixed group of party goers, and we love the people-watching here. If you need a break from the thumping house music or Top 40 beats on the first and second floors, head to the balcony, which is usually reserved for quiet chats and some wind-down time. *1A Nongzhanguan Lu (Chaoyang Park west gate).* ☎ *010/6500-3377. Map p 92.*

Tango DONGCHENG You could get lost in this cavernous nightclub near Ditan Park. Beaded-curtain areas on the second floor offer a great view of the city's 20-some-things on the dance floor. The music ranges from hip-hop to electronica. *Ditan Park south gate.* ☎ *010/6428-2288. Metro: Yonghegong. Map p 92.*

Vic's CHAOYANG This dance club plays a mix of R&B, pop, and soul music. They've also got a "relaxation zone" playing trance music. *Workers' Stadium, north gate.* ☎ *010/6593-6215. Metro: Gongtibeilu. Map p 91.*

★ **White Rabbit** CHAOYANG This recently relocated dance hall has been redesigned to optimize dancing and house music. Known to draw the late-night dance crowd at about 3 or 4am, the dance floor is surrounded by plenty of lounging area to sip on cocktails and absorb loud, pumping music. *2/F-Tongli Studio, Sanlitun Back Street.* ☎ *0/133-2112-3678. Metro: Tuanjiehu. Map p 90.*

Zub HAIDIAN Head here to hang with Beijing's student crowd. This place is run by an Aussie-expat who used to own fitness centers across town. Perhaps that's why there are all those buff young bods shakin' it on the dance floor. *B1/F, Bldg. 12, Huaqing Jia Yuan.* ☎ *010/8286-6420. Metro: Wudaokou. Map p 94.*

Travel Tip

Men beware: Walking along the main bar street, Sanlitun, may require some patience and careful navigation. Bar hawkers often approach foreign-looking men with offers of "lady bars" or "lady services." They

Kala OK

The official Chinese translation of karaoke is kala OK, but everyone calls it KTV. KTV is like the opera—it's an art form that you either love or hate. At first, I belonged to the latter camp. I've always loved singing, but it seemed much too nerdy to admit that I actually liked going to karaoke. But KTV halls in China are nothing like the huge, public karaoke bars we've experienced elsewhere. Here you get your own private room equipped with comfy leather/pleather sofas, a big-screen television, a computer to input songs, and two or three microphones. You can request musical instruments such as tambourines and salsa shakers. Press a button and a service attendant will instantly appear, ready to deliver cold beer or a bottle of whiskey. And as if that weren't enough, a lot of KTV halls come equipped with huge buffets. You can stuff yourself with fried noodles and french fries, or pamper your sore-from-singing throat with chrysanthemum tea between songs. Rocking out to your favorite '80s songs with a close group of friends is a guaranteed night of fun. I love it.

can be very persistent, grabbing at sleeves and tugging. You are unlikely to encounter this if you are out with female companions, but if you're not, keep your eyes straight ahead and simply walk on. Eventually the hawkers will give up.

Gay & Lesbian

★ **Destination** CHAOYANG Beautiful hunky men crowd this sweaty nightclub featuring a busy dance floor. As to be expected from Beijing's best gay club, the music, house and techno, is some of the hottest in town. *7 Gongti Xilu.* ☎ *010/6551-5138. www.bjdestination.com/index_en.htm. Metro: Dongsishitiao. Map p 91.*

Karaoke

Karaoke Partyworld CHAOYANG Like most other Westerners, I used to resist the urge to belt out off-key renditions of Whitney Houston with our Chinese friends and colleagues. Then one night I approached the mic and got hooked. Partyworld is where I get my monthly fix—the multistory emporium offers large private rooms and an extensive menu of English-language tunes. *1/F Fanli Bldg., 22 Chaowai Dajie.* ☎ *010/6588-3333. Private room ¥72–¥190 per hour. Metro: Chaoyang Men. Map p 92.*

Melody CHAOYANG This popular karaoke chain has a decent selection of English songs. *A-77 Chaoyangmenwai Dajie (northwest of Landao Bldg.).* ☎ *010/6551-0808. Private room ¥79–¥189 per hour. Metro: Chaoyangmen. Map p 92.*

Live Music

Cover Charges

Cover charges for the venues listed below vary depending on the musical acts. Prices for bigger-name concerts are usually ¥200 to ¥500. For local bands, prices should be around ¥30 to ¥50.

★ **2 Kolegas** CHAOYANG Its slightly out-of-the-way location, on the grounds of a drive-in movie theater, make this an underground live-music hangout. It's got a nice hippie, happy feel. *21 Liangmaqiao Lu, inside the drive- in movie theater park.* ☎ *010/ 6436-8998. www.2kolegas.com. No metro. Map p 92.*

D-22 HAIDIAN It's a long way from the center of town, but this tight two-floor venue is the best place for experimental music acts. On certain weekdays, the club hosts art house movie nights. *13 Chengfu*

Mesh.

Tango's neon sign.

Lu. ☎ *010/6265-3177. www.d22 beijing.com. Map p 94.*

★ **East Shore Jazz Club** CHAOYANG   Located on the banks of Houhai Lake, this is the perfect place for a romantic drink, as long as you don't mind the crowded, smoky setting. Take a walk around the lake either before or after listening to a jazz set. *2/F, 2 Qianhai Nanyan Lu, Houhai.* ☎ *010/8403-2131. Metro: Gulou. Map p 89.*

Jiangjinjiu Bar DONGCHENG This bar, along the west side of the Drum and Bell Tower, draws a small but loyal crowd of music lovers. The wooden, homey interior is good for a cold pint of Beijing beer and listening to live music, ranging from folk to Mongolian throat singing. *2 Zhongku Alley, west side of the square at Drum and Bell Tower.* ☎ *010/8405-0124. Metro: Gulou. Map p 89.*

★★ **MAO Livehouse** DONGCHENG This live-music venue is backed by the Japanese label Bad News, home of the local punk band Brain Failure. Plenty of aspiring punk rockers have already become loyal fans, to both the band and the bar. *111 Guloudajie.* ☎ *010/6402-5080. Metro: Beixinqiao. Map p 92.*

★ **The Star Live** DONGCHENG The cool music acts (Ziggy Marley, The Roots, Sonic Youth) are finally coming to Beijing, and they seem to like playing at the Star Live. This place is nothing like thumping, downstairs neighbor Tango (p 99); rather, it is small and intimate, with excellent acoustics. *3/F, Tango, 70 Heping Xijie (50m/164 ft. north of subway station).* ☎ *010/6425-5677. www.thestarlive.com. Metro: Yonghegong. Map p 92.*

Yugong Yishan CHAOYANG This longtime music club recently relocated to a swankier setting in a historic building in Beijing's former imperial quarters. It is one of Beijing's best destinations for live music, DJs, rock, jazz, and the occasional international act. You're likely to see lots of trendy Beijing youth loitering outside. *3-2 Zhangzizhong Lu.* ☎ *010/6404-2711 or 010/8402-8477. www.yugongyishan.com. Metro: Zhangzizhonglu. Map p 92.*

Pubs & Sports Bars

Ball House DONGCHENG   Okay, Ball House doesn't screen any sporting events, but it does have a sporty atmosphere to go along with its three pool tables. There are several

KTV (or Karaoke) is extremely popular in Beijing.

lofts and private areas so you can break off in small groups to have private chats. *40 Zhonglouwan (behind and to the left of Hosanna Café).* ☎ *010/6407-4051. Metro: Gulou. Map p 89.*

Black Sun Bar CHAOYANG The closest thing to a neighborhood pub in Beijing, Black Sun Bar offers foosball, a pool table, and darts, along with budget-friendly beers. *Chaoyang Park west gate.* ☎ *010/6593-6909. Map p 92.*

Club Football CHAOYANG This cozy joint has televisions in every corner, and it shows pretty much every sporting event. It's the perfect place to grab a cheap beer, hang out with your mates, and watch a bit of football. They've also got great bar snacks. *10 Chunxiu Lu.* ☎ *010/6416-7786. Metro: Dongzhimen. Map p 92.*

Goose and Duck CHAOYANG Diehard Super Bowl and

sports fans head to this 24-hour bar to watch live games broadcast at unheard-of hours. *Bldg. 1, 105 Yao Jia Yuan Rd.* ☎ *010/5928-3045. www.gdclub.net.cn. Map p 92.*

Red Ball Football Club & Bar CHAOYANG This place has an open-air bar right beside two five-a-side football (soccer) pitches. You can show off how your penalty kick skills are in no way affected by the amount of beer you consume. *Gongti Beilu.* ☎ *010/6413-2848. Metro: Gongtibeilu. Map p 91.*

Wine Bars

Enoteca CHAOYANG If you happen to be in the Central Business District, this wine bar features a decent selection of reds and whites plus a small dinner menu. It's situated in a mall, and I find the setting a little lacking—but that could be said of most of the district! *M102 Northern Tower, The Place, 9A Guanghua Lu.* ☎ *010/6587-1578. www.enoteca.com.cn. Metro: Yonganli. Map p 92.*

★ **Palette Vino** SHUNYI This hard-to-find wine bar, located in the narrow alleys of central Beijing, is worth seeking out for its huge selection of international wines and its intimate setting. The bar also features a nice Continental set menu and sells takeout bottles if you've discovered a new favorite. *5 Dongsi Shiyitiao.* ☎ *010/6405-4855. Metro: Dongsishitiao. Map p 92.*

★★ **Scarlett** CHAOYANG Located in the trendy Hotel G, this wine bar is one of my favorite hangouts in town. They feature a nice selection of European cheeses and main dishes in a brasserie setting with reasonably priced wines. *Hotel G, A7 Gongti Xilu.* ☎ *010/6552-2880. Metro: Chaoyangmen. Map p 91.* ●

Beijing Arts & Entertainment

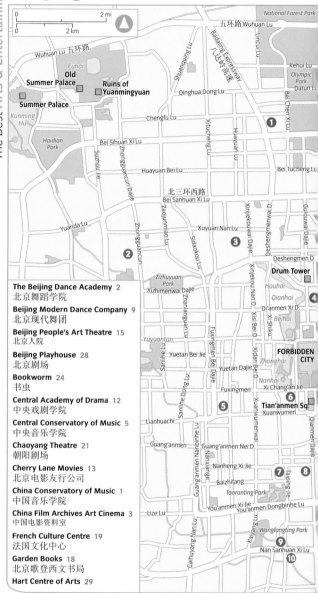

Previous page: The Peking Opera.

Arts & Entertainment Best Bets

Best Acrobat Show
The Beijing Acrobatic Troupe,
Tianqiao Theatre, 95 Tianqiao Market St. (p 107)

Best Brainy Night Out
Bookworm, *4 Sanlitun Nan Lu*
(p 107)

Best Classical Tunes
Central Conservatory of Music,
43 Baojiajie (p 108)

Best Modern Dance Troupe
Beijing Modern Dance Company,
7 West Chang'an Jie (p 109)

Best Place to Spot Rising Stars
Penghao Theater, *35 Dongmianhua*
Hutong, Jiadaokou Nan Dajie (p 112)

Best Place to Meet the Directors of Avant-Garde Films
★ **Cherry Lane Movies,** *3 Zhangzizhong Lu (p 110)*

Best Seasonal Event
★ **Beijing International Festival**
Chorus' Messiah, *Forbidden City*
Concert Hall, Zhongshan Park (p 108)

Best Architecture
National Centre for the Perform-
ing Arts, *West of the Great Hall of*
the People, Tian'anmen Square
(p 109)

Best Traditional Chinese Theater
Peony Pavilion *(p 111)*

Best Traditional Chinese Dance & Chinese Minority Dance
The Beijing Dance Academy, *19*
Minzu Xueyuan Nanlu (p 109)

Discount Tickets

If you wait until the night of a performance, you can often buy high-end tickets for half, or even a quarter, of the face value. Beijing doesn't have a legitimate discount ticket vendor (such as New York's TKTS) that sells day-of tickets to stage events. But if you find yourself without a ticket on the night of a performance you'd love to see, and can't afford the remaining top-end seats, you can usually score a good deal from a scalper. Here's how it works: A lot of high-end tickets are distributed to sponsors or to company employees with no interest in attending the performance. Instead, the recipients head to the venue on the night of the event and sell their tickets cheaply (they got them for free, so it's 100% profit no matter what they get) to the scalpers outside. The scalpers will then try to resell them to passersby or to people looking for a last-minute ticket.

Beijing Arts & Entertainment
A to Z

Acrobats

Chaoyang Theatre CHAOYANG
The centrally located theater is easy to get to, and the Traditional Chinese Acrobatics show's always a hit with visiting family and friends. The show is a standard mix of acrobats twisting themselves into pretzels and soaring through plastic hoops. *36 Dongsanhuan Beilu, Chaoyang Theatre.* ☎ *010/6507-2421. Tickets ¥180–¥680. Map p 104.*

What's Playing?

Two local expatriate magazines, *The Beijinger* and *Time Out* (both monthlies), have excellent up-to-date information regarding the various stage, theater, and music events in town. To buy tickets, try www.piao.com or www.piaowutong.com. These online ticket agents sell tickets to most of the major shows in town and will even deliver them for free if you're staying in central Beijing (within the Second Ring Road).

Tianqiao Acrobatic Theatre

CHAOYANG   The Beijing Acrobatic Troupe is less popular than the show at Chaoyang Theater, but the performances are far better. The century-old theater is a bit worn down, but it's impossible to tear your eyes away from the stage once the show has started. *95 Tianqiao Market St., Tianqiao Acrobatic Theatre.* ☎ *010/6303-7449. Tickets ¥100–¥280. Map p 104.*

Book Events

kids The Bookworm CHAOYANG
The Bookworm has become the de facto community center for downtown expats, who convene here regularly for book talks, musical performances, and open-mic poetry. The cafe also holds kids' book clubs a couple of times a month. *Bldg. 4, Nansanlitun Lu.* ☎ *010/6586-9507. www.beijingbookworm.com. MC, V. Map p 104.*

The skilled acrobats of the Traditional Chinese Acrobatics Show.

Classical Musicians Wanted

Many musical educators in the United States believe that the future of classical music, maybe even its survival, lies in China. China has an estimated 30 million piano students and 10 million violin students. Roughly 200,000 students per year apply for the national music conservatories. And a growing number of these virtuosos are making their way west, lured by scholarships, competitions with lucrative prize money, and opportunities for an international career. Prestigious music schools such as New York's Juilliard and the Eastman School of Music in Rochester have seen a growing number of Chinese-born applicants, and are even sending administrators and directors on scouting trips to China. More and more Western teachers and symphonies are traveling here to teach master classes.

Garden Books CHAOYANG
Smaller and more intimate than the Bookworm is this bookshop, which hosts book talks every month. *44 Guanghua Lu.* ☎ *010/6585-1435. www.gardenbooks.cn. AE, MC, V. Map p 104.*

Classical Music

★ **Beijing International Festival Chorus** This choral group brings together musicians from all over the world and often features visiting guest soloists. Their annual Christmas performance of Handel's *The Messiah* draws a loyal crowd. Check website for venues and upcoming events. *www.beijingifc. org. Tickets ¥50–¥580.*

Beijing Symphony Orchestra
Maestro Tanlihua recently whipped this orchestra into shape. The BSO attaches great importance to China's symphonic music and presents several works by domestic composers. Check the website for venues and upcoming events. *www.bjso.cn. Tickets ¥50–¥320.*

Central Conservatory of Music XICHENG If they're good enough to host Luciano Pavarotti,

Ravi Shankar, and Placido Domingo, they're definitely worth a listen. The Central Conservatory of Music hosts regular performances (many of them free) by students and visiting teachers. *43 Baojiajie.* ☎ *010/6641-2585. en.ccom.edu.cn. Tickets ¥50–¥600. Map p 104.*

China Conservatory of Music
XICHENG Where the Central Conservatory (above) is geared toward

Chaoyang Theatre acrobats.

The National Grand Theater.

classical Western music, this conservatory keeps its ears tuned to traditional Chinese instruments and music styles. *1 Anxiang Lu.* ☎ *010/6641-2585. en.ccom.edu.cn. Tickets ¥50–¥500. Map p 104.*

National Centre for the Performing Arts DONGCHENG   The completion of this much-talked about theater (see p 29, bullet ❶) has been delayed for 3 years. Acoustic tests were scheduled for the summer of 2007, but officials remain tight-lipped about naming the date of the opening performance. *West of the Great Hall of the People, Tian'anmen Square.* ☎ *010/6606-4707. www.chncpa.org. Map p 104.*

Dance
The Beijing Dance Academy HAIDIAN   Walking past the rehearsal halls of this prestigious training academy, you're likely to see ballet, Chinese minority dances, and students goofing around on the barre. Call the office to watch a class, rehearsals, or find out if there is a final class performance scheduled. *19 Minzu Xueyuan Nanlu.*

☎ *010/6893-5691. www.bda.edu. cn. Tickets ¥50–¥300. Map p 104.*

Beijing Modern Dance Company FENGTAI   The *New York Times* called the Beijing Modern Dance Company "the most prominent of Chinese modern dance troupes." Visitors can watch rehearsals; if you're fit, you can even attend a class. *3F, Bldg. D, 46 Fangjia Hutong, Andingmennei Dajie* ☎ *010/6758-0922. www.bmdc.com. cn. Tickets ¥100–¥580. Map p 104.*

The Living Dance Studio CHAOYANG   China's first independent dance-theater company is more performance art than dance. If you're around in the fall, head here to catch its contemporary performance festival, *Crossing*. *105 Caochangdi.* ☎ *010/6533-7243. Tickets ¥50–¥200. Map p 104.*

The National Ballet of China XUANWU   Students from the Beijing Dance Academy (above) feed into this troupe. In the past, their repertoire veered to the uninspired staples of ballet *(Don Quixote, Romeo and Juliet)*, but recent collaborations with international

Members of the National Ballet of China perform for their class in Beijing.

choreographers have livened them up. They perform at various theaters around town. *3 Taipingjie St.* ☎ *010/8355-3737. www.ballet.org. cn. Tickets ¥80–¥680.*

Film (Foreign & Alternative)

★ **Cherry Lane Movies** CHAOY-ANG   Working in conjunction with Yugong Yushan, one of Beijing's best live-music clubs, this movie club shows avant-garde films from Chinese directors (with English subtitles), often with appearances by the directors themselves. *3 Zhangzi-zhong Lu.* ☎ *010/6404-2711. www. cherrylanemovies.com.cn. Tickets ¥50. Map p 104.*

China Film Archives Art Cinema HAIDIAN   If you're in the student district, head to this cinema. They screen Chinese and foreign classics every Thursday at 6:30pm. *Room 1213, 3 Wenhuiyuan Lu, Xia-oxitian.* ☎ *010/6225-4422, ext.*

1214. www.sfa.gov.cn. Tickets ¥25. Map p 104.

French Culture Center CHAOY-ANG   This theater shows classic and modern French films. It's in the French Culture Center, between the bookstore and library, and next to the cafe. *18 Gongti Xilu.* ☎ *010/ 6553-2627. www.ccfpekin.org. Tickets ¥20. Map p 104.*

Hart Centre of Arts CHAOYANG   It feels a bit like a college auditorium, but this center in the 798 Dashanzi Art District shows some of China's most recent avant-garde films with English subtitles on Saturday nights at 7pm. *4 Jiuxianqiao Lu.* ☎ *010/6435-3570. Tickets ¥30. Map p 104.*

Instituto Cervantes CHAOY-ANG   Around the corner from the French Culture Center is, naturally, the Spanish Culture Center. They occasionally screen Spanish films with English subtitles. *1A Gongti Nanlu.* ☎ *010/5879-9666. www.*

pekin.cervantes.es. *Tickets free. Map p 104.*

Italian Embassy Cultural Office

CHAOYANG   This is the place to catch classic and contemporary Italian movies with English subtitles. *2 Sanlitun Donger'jie.* ☎ *010/6532-2187. www.iicpechino.esteri.it. Tickets free. Map p 104.*

Mexican Embassy Cultural Office

CHAOYANG   The Mexican Cultural Office screens Mexican movies with English subtitles. *5 Sanlitun Dongwujie.* ☎ *010/6532-2574. Tickets free. Map p 104.*

Film (Mainstream)

Oriental Plaza Cinema DONG-CHENG   Located in the bustling Oriental Plaza mall (p 66), this large cinema plays Chinese and international blockbusters. *B1-Oriental Plaza, 1 Dong Changan Jie.* ☎ *010/8518-6778. Tickets ¥25–¥70. Metro: Wangfujing. Map p 104.*

★ Sanlitun Village Cinema

CHAOYANG   With many choices for dinner, drinks, and dessert near the cinema, you can make it a full evening at the Village, one of Beijing's newest malls (p 66). *G1, Sanlitun Village.* ☎ *010/6417-6118. www. imegabox.com. Tickets ¥30–¥70. Map p 104.*

Wanda Cinema CHAOYANG   Huge screens and an arcade next door are the main draws at this theater, which plays the standard hits. *3/F, Bldg. B, Wanda Plaza, 93 Jianguo Lu.* ☎ *010/5960-3399. Tickets ¥35–¥120. Map p 104.*

Kung Fu Show

The Red Theatre CHONGWEN   Kung Fu didn't make the cut for the Beijing 2008 Olympics, so you'll have to get your fix here, at "The Legend of Kung Fu." The show features martial arts action that hasn't

been slowed down for the movie cameras. *Red Theatre, 44 Xingfu Dajie.* ☎ *010/6710-3672. Tickets ¥180–¥680. Map p 104.*

Opera

Mei Lanfang Peking Opera Troupe FENGTAI   Mei Lanfang was China's most celebrated modern opera star, and his life story provided the basis for the film *Farewell My Concubine*. The troupe's training is based on Mei's distinctive operatic style. *30 Haihu Xi Li.* ☎ *010/6722-7775. Tickets ¥180–¥380. Map p 104.*

★ Peony Pavilion CHAOYANG

Kunqu opera, a more lyrical offshoot of traditional Peking opera, is offered in this former imperial granary hall, to rave reviews. The performances come with a free dinner buffet. *22 Dongsishitiao, Imperial Granary Theatre, behind Nanxincang Tower.* ☎ *010/6409-6477. Tickets ¥380–¥1,980. Metro: Dongsishitiao Map p 104.*

A Peking Opera performance.

Theater

Beijing People's Art Theatre

DONGCHENG   This is actually a company that has three theaters at its disposal. The main one is Capital Theatre, which stages the company's mainstay, traditional Chinese dramas. *22 Wangfujing St.* ☎ *010/6512-1598. www.bjry.com. Tickets ¥80–¥880. Metro: Dongsi. Map p 104.*

Beijing Playhouse

CHAOYANG   This community theater group performs well-known English-language plays including *The Sound of Music* and *A Christmas Carol. 38 Liangmaqiao Lu.* ☎ *010/6538-4716. www.beijingplayhouse.com.Tickets ¥260–¥400. Map p 104.*

The Central Academy of Drama

DONGCHENG   Famous alumni of the Central Academy of Drama include Zhang Ziyi and Gong Li. Try to spot China's next star at one of their many plays staged at the on-campus theater. *39 Dong Mianhua Hutong.* ☎ *010/6401-7894. www.chntheatre.edu.cn. Tickets ¥50–¥500. Map p 104.*

National Theatre Company of China

DONGCHENG   This hub of young talent has only been around since 2001. They stage classics and contemporary plays. *45 Mao'er Hutong, Di'an Men.* ☎ *010/6403-1009. www.ntcc.com.cn. Tickets ¥50–¥500. Map p 104.*

★★ Penghao Theater

DONGCHENG   This cavernous theater, bar, and restaurant hosts renditions of Western and Chinese classics. Located near the Central Academy of Drama (see above), this theater has been a magnet for artists who live and work around the area. *35 Dongmianhua Hutong, Jiadaokou Nan Dajie.* ☎ *010/6400-6472. www. penghaoren.com/cn. Tickets ¥50–¥160. Map p 104.*

TNT (The Nine Theatres)

CHAOYANG   TNT doesn't have a resident theater group, but this is a great venue where you can catch regular performances in any one of the three main theaters. Their goal is to eventually have nine theaters, hence their name. *17 Jintaili, Chaoyangmenwai.* ☎ *010/8599-6011. www.ninetheater.com. Tickets ¥100–¥500. Map p 104.* ●

Peking Opera performers.

Lodging Best Bets

Best **Boutique Hotel**
★★ Opposite House $$$$$ *11 Sanlitun Bei Lu (p 126)*

Most **Intimate**
★ Du Ge $$$$$ *26 Qianyuanensi Hutong (p 123)*

Most **Historic**
★★ Bamboo Garden Hotel $$ *24 Xiaoshiqiao (p 121)*; and ★★ Han's Royal Garden Hotel $$$$ *7 Bei Bingmasi Hutong (p 125)*

Best for a **Weekend Getaway**
★★ Aman Resort $$$$$ *15 Gongmenqian Lu (p 120)*

Best **Hutong Hideaway**
★ Courtyard 7 $$$ *7 Qian Gulou Yuan Hutong (p 122)*

Best **Bargain**
Beijing Downtown Backpackers Accommodations $ *85 Nan Luogu Xiang (p 121)*

Best **Design**
★★ Commune at the Great Wall $$$$ *Exit at Shuiguan, Badaling Hwy. (p 122)*; and ★★ Opposite House $$$$$ *11 Sanlitun Bei Lu (p 126)*

Best **Countryside Getaway**
★★ Commune at the Great Wall $$$$ *Exit at Shuiguan, Badaling Hwy. (p 122)*; and ★ Red Capital Ranch $$$$ *28 Xiaguandi Cun, Yanxi Zhen (p 127)*

Best **Health & Fitness Facilities**
★★ Park Hyatt $$$$$ *2 Jianguomen Wai Dajie (p 126)*; and ★★ Aman Beijing $$$$$ *15 Gongmenqian Lu (p 120)*

Best **Splurge Hotel**
★★ Park Hyatt $$$$$ *2 Jianguomen Wai Dajie (p 126)*; and ★★ Aman Beijing $$$$$ *15 Gongmenqian Lu (p 120)*

Best **Service Apartment**
★ The Ascott $$$$ *108 Jianguo Lu Yi (p 120)*

Best **Newcomer**
★★ Opposite House $$$$$ *11 Sanlitun Bei Lu (p 126)*

Most **Comfortable Beds**
★★ Ritz-Carlton Financial Street $$$$ *1 Jinchengfang Dong Jie (p 129)*

A room at the Commune's "Distorted Courtyard." Previous page: A room at the Red Capital Ranch.

Central Business District Lodging

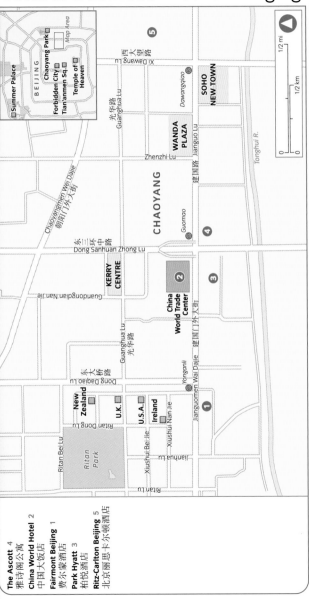

The Ascott 4
雅诗阁公寓

China World Hotel 2
中国大饭店

Fairmont Beijing 1
费尔蒙酒店

Park Hyatt 3
柏悦酒店

Ritz-Carlton Beijing 5
北京丽思卡尔顿酒店

Wangfujing Lodging

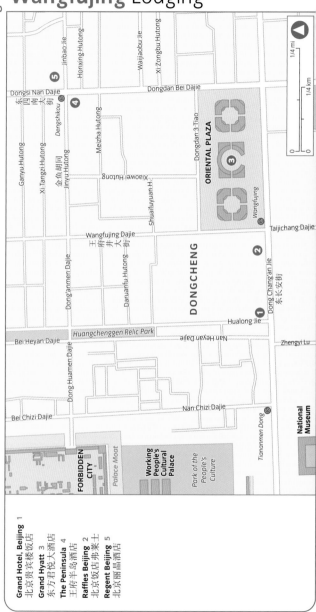

Grand Hotel, Beijing 1
北京贵宾楼饭店

Grand Hyatt 3
东方君悦大酒店

The Peninsula 4
王府半岛酒店

Raffles Beijing 2
北京饭店弗莱士

Regent Beijing 5
北京丽晶酒店

Houhai Lake Area Lodging

Bamboo Garden Hotel 3
竹园宾馆

Drum Tower Youth Hostel 5
鼓楼青年酒店

Qomolangma Hotel 2
珠穆朗玛宾馆

7 Days Inn 4
7天连锁酒店

Sleepy Inn 1
丽舍什刹海国际青年旅舍

Beijing Lodging

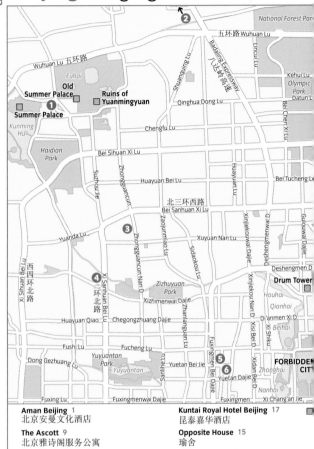

Nan Luogu Xiang Lodging

Drum Tower

Gulou Dong Dajie

Tu'er Hutong

Ju'er Hutong

Qian Gulou
Yuan Hutong

Jiaodaokou Nan Dajie

Qian Yuan Insi
Hutong

Qintao Hutong

Mao'er Hutong

Bei Bingmasi
Hutong

Nanluogu Xiang

Di'anmenwai Dajie

Houhai
Lake

Qianhai Nan Yan

Banchang Hutong

Di'anmen Dong Dajie

0   1/4 mi

0   1/4 km

Di'anmennei Dajie

Gongjian Hutong

Huanghuamen Jie

Jingshan Houjie

Jingshan
Park

Dong Banqiao Jie

**Beijing Downtown Backpackers
Accommodation** 4
东堂客栈

Courtyard 7 2
7号院

Du Ge 3
杜革四合院艺术精品酒店

Gu Xiang 20 1
古巷20号

Han's Royal Garden Hotel 5
北京涵珍园国际酒店

Lu Song Yuan 6
侣松园宾馆

Beijing Hotels A to Z

★★ Aman Beijing HAIDIAN
Wood floors, high ceilings, and
Ming-style furniture decorate the
luxurious rooms in this beautiful
resort, located right in the gates of
the Summer Palace. Rooms come
with private access to the palace,
and amenities include a world-class
spa, a movie theater, and a Pilates
studio. It's a trek from the center of
town, but worthwhile for a couple of
nights if you want to get away from
the hubbub of downtown and see
northwest Beijing's sights. *15 Gongmenqian Lu.* ☎ *010/5987-9999. 51
units. Doubles ¥3,700–¥4,500. AE,
DISC, MC, V. Map p 118.*

★ kids The Ascott CHAOYANG and
DONGCHENG   With two locations in

central Beijing, this serviced apartment hotel is a good choice for
extended trips or if you've got kids
in town. Rooms come with fully
equipped kitchens and up to three
bedrooms. There's not a whole lot of
character in the decor but the amenities and service make up for it. *Location in Chaoyang (in the Central
Business District): 108 Jianguo Lu Yi.*
☎ *010/6567-8100 or 800/820-1028.
www.the-ascott.com. 310 units. Doubles ¥1,688, plus 15% service charge;
breakfast for one included in rate. AE,
DISC, MC, V. Metro: Guomao. Map
p 115. Location in Dongcheng (closer
to the airport): 1–2 Dongzhimen Da Jie.*
☎ *010/8405-3888 or 800/820-1028.
www.the-ascott.com. 192 units. Doubles ¥1,088, plus 15% service charge.*

AE, DISC, MC, V. Metro: Dongzhimen.
Map p 118.

★★ Bamboo Garden Hotel

DONGCHENG This courtyard
guesthouse is the place to live out
your dowager or emperor of China
fantasies. The traditional compound
was once the garden of a high-rank-
ing Qing dynasty eunuch. Red lac-
quer walkways lead the way to
rooms decked out in Ming dynasty
style. An extra sitting area and
larger bathroom make the deluxe
suites well worth the upgrade. *24
Xiaoshiqiao (off Jiugulou Dajie).*
☎ *010/5852-0088. www.bbgh.com.
cn. 60 units. Doubles ¥760–¥880. AE,
MC, V. Metro: Gulou. Map p 117.*

★ Beijing Downtown Back-packers Accommodation

DONGCHENG This is by far the
best hostel in Beijing and it's in a
fabulous location. They have bar-
gain-basement dorm rooms (¥55) as
well as private singles and doubles.
The bathroom has that annoying
layout with a toilet placed smack in
the middle of the shower area, but it
is very clean and the folks at the
reception desk speak excellent English. *85 Nan Lougu Xiang.* ☎ *010/
8400-2429. 20 units. Doubles ¥150–
¥190 w/breakfast. No credit cards.
Map p 120.*

Sitting area at Beijing Backpackers.

★ China World Hotel

Once
one of the top hotels in Beijing, this
hotel now needs a renovation to
compete with Beijing's newer five-
star hotels. Yet it remains quite popular with high-end business
travelers for its central location in
the Central Business District. You
should be able to bargain down the
price; otherwise, stay elsewhere. *1
Jianguomen Wai Dajie, Chaoyang
District.* ☎ *010/6505-2266. www.
shangri-la.com. 716 units. Doubles
¥1,700–¥1,900. AE, DISC, MC, V.
Metro: Guomao. Map p 115.*

The relaxing surroundings at Bamboo Garden.

How to Choose a Hotel

Beijing's sprawling size and large number of hotels can make it difficult to decide where to stay. If you're planning to visit popular attractions and want to get a feel for Old Beijing, try to stay in one of the hutong neighborhoods within the Dongcheng district. Good choices include Han Royal Garden Hotel, Guxiang 20, Bamboo Garden, and Courtyard 7. If you want to be in the main hub of tourist activity but prefer the comforts of a luxury hotel, try the Peninsula, the Grand Hyatt, or the Regent. The Central Business District is of course great for people who are here to do business with Fortune 500 companies, and it's reasonably close to most of Beijing's attractions. The northwest part of town, Haidian, is the university district and Beijing's Silicon Valley. It is also home to the Summer Palace and near Fragrant Hills. If you stay here, however, you'll be an hour's taxi ride away from main attractions such as Tian'anmen Square and the Forbidden City. The newest district is Financial Street, where an outpost of The Ritz-Carlton and The Westin are located (each brand also has properties on the east side of town, in and around the Central Business District). Fairly close to Tian'anmen Square and the Forbidden City, these hotels mainly draw an investment banking clientele.

★★ kids **Commune at the Great Wall** BADALING   This hotel's stunning architecture and location near the Great Wall make it a perfect place to retreat from the city. The Commune's 12 original villas, designed by international architects, are often rented for lavish parties. Copies of the homes have been subdivided into more affordable hotel rooms. A large kid's club offers free babysitting and an outdoor wading pool. See p 134, bullet ❷. *Exit at Shuiguan, Badaling Hwy.* ☎ *010/8118-1888. www.commune. com.cn. 201units. Doubles ¥2,700 w/breakfast. AE, MC, V. Map p 118.*

Confucius International Youth Hostel CHAOYANG   This hostel is right in the thick of things on up-and-coming Wudaoying Hutong, a lively alley that has seen a slew of cafes, restaurants, and boutiques

open in the last year. Rooms are basic, but a good size. *38 Wudaoying Hutong.* ☎ *010/6402-2082 or 0/139-1076-9159. 16 units. Doubles ¥200. No credit cards. Metro: Yonghegong. Map p 118.*

★ **Courtyard 7** CHAOYANG Located just off the very popular alley Nan Luogu Xiang, this boutique hotel in a traditional courtyard dwelling offers cozy rooms decorated with Chinese antiques and white curtained windows overlooking one of several central gardens. *7 Qian Gulou Yuan Hutong.* ☎ *010/ 6406-0777. 19 units. Doubles ¥1,180–¥1,900. AE, DISC, MC, V. Metro: Beixinqiao. Map p 120.*

Drum Tower Youth Hostel DONGCHENG   This is a great place to crash if you are on a budget. The rooms and bathrooms are small, but the prices are rock bottom. *51 Jiu*

A hideaway bed at the Commune's Suitcase House.

Gulou Dajie, Xicheng District. ☎ 010/
6403-7702. www.guyunhostel.com.
50 units. Dorm Beds ¥45–¥55. Doubles ¥170. AE, MC, V. Metro: Gulou.
Map p 117.

★ **kids** **Du Ge** CHAOYANG This
posh, cozy 10-room boutique hotel
sitting right off of the popular alley
of Nan Luogu Xiang is a sign of Beijing's rapidly gentrifying times. Lacquered furniture in bright colors has
been custom made and fitted, while
fancy touches including crystal
chandeliers and antique carpets
round out the polished, flashy feel

of the rooms. The hotel also features separate rooms designed
for kids. *26 Qianyuanensi Hutong.
☎ 010/6406-0686. 10 units. Doubles
¥1,200–¥3,000. AE, DISC, MC, V.
Metro: Beixinqiao. Map p 120.*

The Emperor CHAOYANG Down
a shady lane right next to the Forbidden City, this four-story boutique
hotel offers unique rooms in a fabulous location. Beds and sofas are
built into each room's white walls
streaked with bright textured fabric
in a single color of turquoise blue,
lime green, or bright orange, giving
the rooms a futuristic, stylish feel.
*33 Qihelou Jie. ☎ 800-3746-8357 or
010/6526-5566. 55 units. Doubles
¥1,000–¥1,400. AE, DISC, MC, V.
Metro: Dengshikou or Tian'anmen
Dong. Map p 118.*

★ **Fairmont Beijing** CHAOYANG
One of Beijing's newest luxury
hotels, the Fairmont's location in the
Central Business District makes it a
good choice for businesspeople or
finicky leisure travelers looking for
plush rooms and suites loaded with
amenities. The hotel's spa is one of
the most luxurious in town. *8 Yongan Dong Li, Jianguomen Wai Dajie.
☎ 010/8511-777 or 866/551-5659.
222 units. Doubles ¥2,700–¥30,000.
AE, MC, V. Metro: Yonganli. Map
p 115.*

Fairmont Beijing.

★ **kids** **Friendship Hotel** HAIDIAN   If you want a feel of what Beijing was like in the 1960s, this enormous hotel complex—with sprawling grounds and an outdoor swimming pool—is the place to go. The hotel once housed Soviet foreign experts and features Soviet-Chinese architecture, but recent updates to the rooms have given them a modern, hip feel. The hotel is convenient for those who want to be near the Summer Palace and Beijing's version of Silicon Valley. *1 Zhongguancun Nan Dajie.* ☎ *010/6849-8888. www.bjfriendshiphotel. com. 2,300 units. Doubles ¥500–¥700. AE, MC, V. Metro: Remin Daxue. Map p 118.*

Friendship Youth Hostel CHAOYANG   Four bars surround one side of this hostel and the other side faces a pub. Lodgings here are bare-bones basic—rooms are small and bathrooms are shared with fellow floor mates. *43 Beisanlitun Nan.* ☎ *010/6417-2632. www.poachers.com.cn. Doubles ¥200. MC, V. Map p 118.*

★ **Grand Hotel, Beijing** DONGCHENG   This hotel, just past the northeast corner of Tian'anmen Square, is the closest you can stay to the square. Foreign journalists camped out here during the 1989 massacre; today it's a luxury hotel with nicely appointed rooms. *35 East Chang'an Jie.* ☎ *010/6513-7788. www.grandhotelbeijing.com. 217 units. Doubles ¥1,600–¥2,200. AE, MC, V. Metro: Wangfujing. Map p 116.*

★★ **Grand Hyatt** DONGCHENG   The smaller-than-average rooms are efficiently designed, but the real draw here is the amenities, including the pool, which boasts a surreal tropical setting. The hotel also serves some of the best food in town in its restaurant, Made in China (p 81). *1 Dong Chang'an Jie.* ☎ *010/8518-1234. www.beijing.grand.hyatt.com. 825 units. Doubles ¥2,000–¥3,800. AE, DISC, MC, V. Metro: Wangfujing. Map p 116.*

★ **Gu Xiang 20** DONGCHENG   This intimate hotel located on a bar-lined alley in the hutongs (near my home) boasts modern rooms decorated with Chinese antiques and flatscreen TVs. *20 Nan Luogu Xiang.*

The swimming pool at the Grand Hyatt.

Han's Royal Garden.

010/6400-5566. www.guxiang20. com. 28 units. Doubles ¥500–¥1,280. AE, DISC, MC, V. Metro: Beixinqiao. Map p 120.

★★ Han's Royal Garden Hotel

CHAOYANG   A collaboration between a wealthy Chinese American and the grandson of a Qing dynasty chef, this painstakingly restored series of five courtyards has been turned into a luxurious hotel with an emphasis on preserving China's history and culture. Most rooms are decorated comfortably with expensive yet understated dark wood furniture with a Western feel, while the more lavish rooms have been filled with antique Chinese rosewood furniture. *7 Bei Bingmasi Hutong.* ☎ *010/8402-5588. 33 units. Doubles ¥1,180–¥1,900. AE, DISC, MC, V. Metro: Zhangzizhonglu. Map p 120.*

Hejing Fu Binguan DONGCHENG

This hotel was built on the site of Qing dynasty Hefing Princess's former mansion. Today it smells a bit stale and the bathrooms have seen better days. The traditional courtyards (private, single-level traditional houses with rooms set around a central "courtyard" space) in front of the hotel were under renovation at press time. The courtyards look more charming than the hotel itself, and will be worth checking out

when renovations are complete. *7 Zhang Zi Zhonglu.* ☎ *010/6401-7744. 140 units. Doubles ¥400–¥960. AE, MC, V. Metro: Zhangzizhonglu. Map p 118.*

★ Hotel G CHAOYANG   Part of

the growing boutique hotel trend in Beijing, Hotel G offers stylish rooms done up in a "1960's Hollywood" glamour theme in a central location that's right near much of Beijing's pulsating nightlife. There's a whimsical touch, with rubber duckies near the tub and toy motorcycles decorating the rooms, which also come with all the modern technology you'll need, including an iPod dock and flatscreen television. *A7 Gongti Xi Lu.* ☎ *010/6552-3600. 110 units. Doubles ¥1,088–¥1,288. AE, DISC, MC, V. Metro: Chaoyangmen. Map p 118.*

★ Kuntai Royal Hotel Beijing

CHAOYANG   This Chinese-run hotel features plush rooms with wood walls and staff members who speak decent English. The location is conveniently situated midpoint between the Central Business District and many of Beijing's attractions. *12 Chaoyangmen Wai Dajie Yi.* ☎ *010/5828-5588. www.kuntai royalhotel.com. 358 units. Doubles ¥1,800–¥2,900. AE, DISC, MC, V. Map p 118.*

A bedroom at Lu Song Yuan.

Lu Song Yuan DONGCHENG
This midrange hotel, owned by an enterprising Hong Kong business-man who owns several boutique hotels around China, has a prime location in the hutongs and plenty of character. Its dimly lit rooms are decorated with Chinese antiques and the building was once the home of a Qing dynasty general. *22 Ban-chang Hutong, Kuan Jie.* ☎ *010/ 6404-0436. www.the-silk-road.com/ hotel/lusongyuanhotel. 55 units. Doubles ¥700–¥1,000. AE, MC, V. Map p 120.*

Park Hyatt Beijing.

★★ Opposite House CHAOY-ANG   Located on the Sanlitun bar street, this classy boutique hotel represents how far this once-scummy area (and Beijing as a whole) has come. You won't expect much from the boring glass exterior, but once inside, everything is styl-ish, from the open atrium lobby featuring Chinese modern art instal-lations to the stainless-steel-bot-tomed pool in the basement. Rooms are decorated in minimalist white and blond wood tones. The only drawback is the hefty price tag. *11 Sanlitun Bei Lu.* ☎ *010/6417-6688. 99 units. Doubles ¥5,000–¥6,500. AE, DISC, MC, V. Metro: Gongtibeilu. Map p 118.*

Park Hyatt CHAOYANG   Rising above the area known as the CBD—the Central Business District—this new 66-story hotel impresses with expansive views of the city, top-notch gym and spa facilities, and unconventional room layouts deco-rated in beige tones. Most rooms open into an airy bathroom, outfit-ted with marble tubs next to an open shower, a freestanding his-and-hers sink and mirror, and a sliding door that separates the bath-room from the sleeping quarters

beyond. *2 Jianguomenwai Dajie.* ☎ *010/8567-1234. www.beijing. park.hyatt.com. 237 units. Doubles ¥2,000–¥2,500. AE, MC, V. Metro: Guomao. Map p 115.*

★★ **The Peninsula** DONGCHENG At Beijing's most luxurious hotel, the spacious rooms come with flatscreen televisions, DVD players, and tasteful contemporary Chinese art. The service is top-notch, and nearly every staff member speaks fluent English. The Pen even gets the details right, as in the easy-to-use lighting system and evening turndown service. Make sure to book a room with a television in the bathroom so you can bathe while watching a movie from the hotel's library. This hotel also holds Beijing's fanciest shopping arcade, with three floors of designer names such as Chanel and Harry Winston. *8 Jinyu Hutong, Wangfujing.* ☎ *010/ 8516-2888, or 800/852-3888 for calls from Beijing. http://beijing.peninsula. com. 525 units. Doubles ¥2,800. AE, DISC, MC, V. Map p 116.*

★ **Qomolangma Hotel** DONG-CHENG At the rear of the Qomolangma is a vast courtyard containing four other separate and private courtyards. Make sure to request a room here, rather than in the street-facing building, which is just a regular hotel. Courtyard rooms are furnished with traditional Chinese furniture, and the deluxe suites come with big bathtubs. *149 Gulou Xi Dajie.* ☎ *010/6401-8822. www.qomolangma hotel.com. 81 units. Doubles ¥ 780– ¥2,880. AE, MC, V. Metro: Gulou. Map p 117.*

Raffles Beijing DONGCHENG If you're familiar with the Raffles in Singapore, this Beijing outpost, which opened in 2006, may be a disappointment. While the historic building has been restored carefully, the rooms are tacky, with mismatched carpets and furniture upholstery. The small balconies look out onto Chang'an Jie, one of Beijing's main thoroughfares. *33 Dong Chang'an Jie.* ☎ *010/6526-3388 or 800/768-9009. www.beijing.raffles.com. 171 units. Doubles ¥3,800–¥4,700. AE, DISC, MC, V. Metro: Wangfujing. Map p 116.*

★ **Red Capital Ranch** HUAIROU An 80-minute drive from Beijing, this country guesthouse, owned by the Red Capital Residence, is the perfect weekend retreat. The high-ceilinged rooms with stone walls feature Qing dynasty–style furniture. Don't expect too much in terms of service; the place is staffed with young countryside women. The ranch is closed in the winter months. *28 Xiaguandi Cun, Yanxi Zhen, Huairou District.* ☎ *010/8401-8886. www.red capitalclub.com.cn. 10 units. Doubles ¥1,540 w/breakfast. AE, MC, V. Map p 118.*

★★ **Regent Beijing** DONGCHENG Everything about this hotel is elegant and understated, from the muted beige and gray tones of the rooms to the swimming pool lined

The lobby at Raffles Beijing.

Countryside Getaways

Whenever we're feeling overwhelmed by Beijing's pollution, traffic, and crowds, we head for the mountains. Just a little over an hour outside Beijing are two countryside resorts that make excellent overnight trips. The Red Capital Ranch (p 127), an 80-minute drive from downtown, is just under an unrestored section of the Great Wall. Its ten rooms are in private Chinese-style bungalows decorated with Tibetan and Chinese antiques. The charm of the rooms lies in its details—such as the decorative Chinese chessboards on the walls of the bathroom—but the bugs crawling around are a powerful reminder that you are indeed in the country. While most guests come here to relax in the outdoor pavilions, at the spa, or by the cozy fireplace, the resort also offers a challenging hike along the Great Wall. This section of the Wall has mostly been reduced to rubble, and it makes for a rigorous climb that meanders along a ridge of rocks and ends in a sheer cliff drop on which an old watchtower teeters. The hike is 4 hours long, round-trip. Another option is the **Commune** (p 122 and 134), which offers more luxurious accommodations and an easier climb on an unrestored but more intact section of the Wall.

with slate-gray stone floors and walls. The rooms are spacious and outfitted with flatscreen televisions and DVD players. The price for the executive suites includes a complimentary 30-minute massage. *99 Jinbao Jie, Dongcheng District.* ☎ *010/8522-1888.* *www.regenthotels.com. 500 units. Doubles ¥1,800–¥2,750. AE, DISC, MC, V. Metro: Dengshikou. Map p 116.*

You can enjoy a weekend away from the city at the Red Capital Ranch.

The swimming pool at the St. Regis.

★★ **Ritz-Carlton Beijing** CHAOY-ANG   Not to be confused with the *other* new Ritz-Carlton on the other side of town, this new five-star hotel sits just east of Beijing's CBD (Central Business District) and comes with impressive service and a distinctly old-world, European feel. While rooms have a classic look with flowery throw pillows and dark wood furniture, they're also outfitted with modern technology including iPod docks, flatscreen televisions, and Wi-Fi. *38 Jianguo Lu.* ☎ *010/5908-8888. 305 units. Doubles ¥4,800–¥5,800. AE, DISC, MC, V. Metro: Dawanglu. Map p 115.*

★★ **Ritz-Carlton Financial Street** XICHENG   Though this Ritz caters to a business clientele, it is rife with homey touches, as if it had been decorated by a Chinese Martha Stewart. The beds are the comfiest in town, and the marble bathrooms come with two sinks and a television anchored in front of the bathtub. The basement health club has a luxurious swimming pool with a giant television screen on one wall, plus lounge chairs that deliver water jet massages. Cepe, on the ground level, serves the city's best upscale Italian fare. This hotel's only

drawback is its location, which isn't particularly central, though it's convenient enough to the Forbidden City and Tian'anmen Square. *1 Jinchengfang Dong Jie, Xicheng District.* ☎ *010/6601-6666. www.ritz-carlton.com. 253 units. Doubles ¥4,500–¥5,000. AE, DISC, MC, V. Metro: Fuchengmen. Map p 118.*

7 Days Inn DONGCHENG   It may look like a parking lot motel, but this newly opened inn is immaculate and has an extremely friendly staff. Bathrooms have separate shower areas and the south-facing top floor rooms have decent views of the Bell Tower. *47 Jiugulou Dajie.* ☎ *010/6405-8188. www.7daysinn.com. 159 units. Doubles ¥240. No credit cards. Metro: Gulou. Map p 117.*

★ **Shangri-La** HAIDIAN   Standard rooms in the older tower are comfortable, but slightly worn—for an extra ¥500, it's worthwhile to upgrade to the Valley Wing, a luxurious tower of new executive rooms decorated in elegant muted beige tones, with access to an indulgent lounge with free breakfast, afternoon cocktails, and canapés. Its location puts you a 30-minute drive from many of Beijing's tourist attractions, but the hotel is close to the university district. *29 Zizhuyuan Lu.* ☎ *010/6841-2211. www.shangri-la. com. 528 units. Doubles ¥1,050–¥1,800. AE, DISC, MC, V. Map p 118.*

★ **Sleepy Inn** DONGCHENG This budget lakeside inn has some of the friendliest service in Beijing. Rooms on the northern end of the compound look out over Xihai Lake. Amenities are basic, but the rooms and bathrooms are spick-and-span. *103 Deshengmen Nei Dajie.* ☎ *010/ 6406-9954. www.sleepyinn.com.cn. 24 units. 4-person dorms ¥80 per person. Doubles ¥298. No credit cards. Metro: Gulou. Map p. 117.*

★ **St. Regis** CHAOYANG It was once the best hotel in town, but the St. Regis no longer stands out as the front-runner with so many new five-star hotels vying for attention. Still, rooms are homey and comfortable, with Chinese touches, modern Bose speakers, big flatscreen televisions, and DVD players. Beds are plush and feature high-thread-count sheets, and bathrooms have been made fancy with white marble. *21 Jianguomen Wai Dajie.* ☎ *010/6460-6688 or 800/810-3288. www.stregis. com/beijing. 273 units. Doubles ¥4,100–¥5,000. AE, DISC, MC, V. Metro: Jianguomen. Map p 118.*

★ **Swissôtel** CHAOYANG An older five-star hotel, the Swissôtel is often overlooked. But its convenient location (midway between the airport and Beijing's Central Business District), no-nonsense rooms, and professional service make it a good value. *2 Chaoyangmen Bei Dajie.* ☎ *010/6553-2288. www.beijing. swissotel.com. 430 units. Doubles ¥1,100–¥1,700 w/breakfast. AE, MC, V. Metro: Dongsi Shitiao. Map p 118.*

★★ **The Westin Beijing Chaoyang** XICHENG One of Beijing's newest five-star hotels, this second Westin to open in the capital offers stylish, modern rooms in a fairly central location with quick access to the airport. It was Hillary Clinton's choice when she made her first visit to China as secretary of state (the U.S. embassy is located just a few blocks away). *1 Xinyuan Nan Lu.* ☎ *010/5922-8888 or 800/810-3688. www.westin.com/chaoyang. 550 units. Doubles ¥2,500–¥4,000. AE, DISC, MC, V. Metro: Liangmaqiao. Map p 118.*

★ kids **The Westin Financial Street** XICHENG Located on the west side of town, this Westin caters to a business clientele and those traveling with children. The rooms are comfortable, if a little characterless, but you'll get all the services and amenities that come with the brand name. *9 Jinrong Jie Yi.* ☎ *010/ 6606-8866 or 800/810-3688. www. westin.com/beijingfinancial. 486 units. Doubles ¥2,900. AE, DISC, MC, V. Metro: Fuchengmen. Map p 118.* ●

A cozy bed at Swiss Road.

The **Great Wall & the Commun**

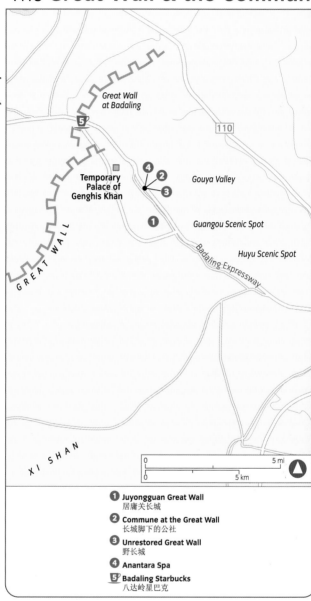

Great Wall at Badaling

110

Gouya Valley

Temporary Palace of Genghis Khan

Guangou Scenic Spot

Huyu Scenic Spot

Badaling Expressway

X I   S H A N

0   5 mi

0   5 km

1 **Juyongguan Great Wall**
居庸关长城

2 **Commune at the Great Wall**
长城脚下的公社

3 **Unrestored Great Wall**
野长城

4 **Anantara Spa**

5 **Badaling Starbucks**
八达岭星巴克

Previous page: Chengde.

While the sections of the Great Wall that we recommend in this tour are not far from Badaling (p 137)—the most commercial and most visited part of the wall—they couldn't be more different. This day-long tour will give you an insider's peek at two peaceful parts of the Wall, plus take you to one of China's most avant-garde architectural projects where you can enjoy post-climb pampering at a spa.

Travel Tips

The 1-hour journey to the Commune and the other points mentioned on this tour can be made by taxi or bus (tourist bus no. 1 or 5 from Qianmen or tourist bus no. 2 from Beijing Railway Station will take you to Juyongguan), but our recommendation is that you rent a car for the day (p 155). If you overnight at the Commune (highly recommended, p 134), the hotel can arrange return transport to the city or drop you off at the Badaling Bus Station if you'd prefer to avoid the costly transfer fee.

1 ★★ Juyongguan Great Wall.
The Juyongguan section of the Great Wall, a recently restored area an hour away from downtown Beijing, is one of the sections closest to the city

and the most historically significant. Guarding one of two crucial passes to Beijing and the North China Plain, it was the site of pitched battles involving Jurchen, Mongol, and Japanese invaders. There may have been fortifications here as early as the 6th century—before Beijing existed. (Ironically, the name Juyongguan means Dwelling in Harmony Pass.) In any case, it affords breathtaking views—our professional photographer friends agree that it's their favorite section of the Wall. Yet Juyongguan receives fewer tourists than other areas, making for a peaceful climb. It's worth stopping at Juyongguan to view the ancient and remarkable Yun Tai (Cloud Platform), which once stood astride the old road running northwest into Mongol territories. Dating from 1342, it was the base for three Tibetan-style stupas,

The Juyongguan Pass section of the Great Wall.

The Outside of See and Be Seen, one of the Commune houses.

which were toppled by an earthquake and replaced during the Ming dynasty by a Buddhist temple. 🕐 *2 hr. Juyongguan Great Wall.* ☎ *010/6977-1665. Admission ¥45. Daily 8am–5pm. Bus 919 from Deshengmen to Nankou Dong Jie, then transfer to bus 68 to Juyongguan.*

❷ ★★★ Commune at the Great Wall. One of China's most avant-garde architectural projects, the Commune assembles the work of 12 established architects, mostly from Asia, who were given tracts of land near the Great Wall to build their dream homes. The homes are sometimes occupied by those who can afford the high daily rental fees, but if the homes are empty, they can be toured. In 2006, the Commune built copies of the original homes on the same plot of land and subdivided them into boutique hotel rooms. This is the perfect retreat from the city if you're craving some country air. *One catch is that the*

The Houses of the Commune

Developers Zhang Xin and Pan Shiyi gave the countryside near Beijing a face-lift when they commissioned a dozen architects to build fanciful homes here in 2001. A paved street meanders up a dry, dusty hill, passing homes of varied colors and unusual shapes. Not far from the main gate is the **Suitcase House,** which consists of a large room with hinged wooden floors that when lifted reveal hidden rooms including a bedroom, kitchen, and bathroom. Farther up the road is another one of our favorites, the **Airport House,** which resembles an airport terminal with jutting corridors that function as rooms rather than airport boarding gates. Next up is the serene **Bamboo Wall House,** a long house constructed from thin, delicate bamboo. It features an outdoor dining area surrounded by water. Another of our favorites is the **Forest House,** which has large vertical windows and meandering, airy hallways that give the house the depth of a labyrinth, without feeling claustrophobic.

hotel only allows guests to scale the property's section of the Great Wall—you can get around this by having a drink or dining here and then going for a stroll. 🕐 *1 hr. Exit at Shuiguan, Badaling Hwy.* ☎ *010/ 8118-1888, ext. 4. Free for guests. Daily tour: 9am–5pm (by appointment).*

③ **★★ Unrestored Great Wall.** Besides the cool architecture, another good reason to come to the Commune is so you can explore their unrestored, private section of the Wall. Follow the path next to the red Cantilever House (on the right, if you're facing the house), keeping on the trail. The hike isn't too rigorous for nonhikers, but it can be steep at points, so be sure to wear good shoes. 🕐 *1 hr.*

An unrestored section of the Great Wall near the Commune.

Relax after your long walk at the Commune's spa.

④ **★ Anantara Spa.** If you've walked the two sections of the Great Wall recommended in this tour, you may be ready for a body treatment or a foot massage at this elegant spa. The spa has an outdoor deck with a perfect view of the wall on clear days. 🕐 *1 hr. Exit at Shuiguan, Badaling Hwy., located in the Commune at the Great Wall.* ☎ *010/8118-1888, ext. 5100 (by appointment).*

⑤ **Badaling Starbucks.** The touts and crowds at the Badaling section of the Great Wall can be a bit overwhelming, but we are willing to brave them for a cup of coffee. This Starbucks is the only coffee shop within a 48km (30-mile) radius. *Opposite the entrance at the Great Wall, Badaling Changcheng Tequ, Yanqing.* ☎ *010/6912-1894. $.*

More **Great Wall Excursions**

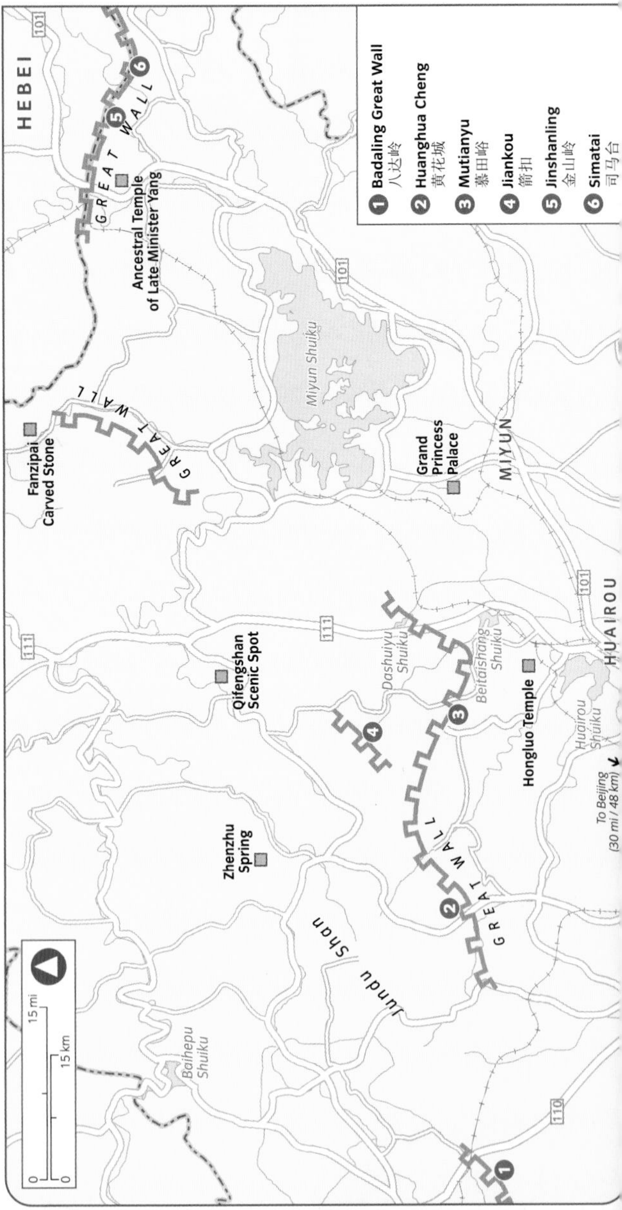

1 Badaling Great Wall
八达岭

2 Huanghua Cheng
黄花城

3 Mutianyu
慕田峪

4 Jiankou
箭扣

5 Jinshanling
金山岭

6 Simatai
司马台

HEBEI

GREAT WALL

Ancestral Temple
of Late Minister Yang

Miyun Shuiku

GREAT WALL

Fanzipai
Carved Stone

Grand
Princess
Palace

MIYUN

HUAIROU

101

101

111

111

110

110

Qifengshan
Scenic Spot

Daoshuyu
Shuiku

Beidishang
Shuiku

Honglo Temple

Huairou
Shuiku

To Beijing
(30 mi / 48 km)

Zhenzhu
Spring

Jundu Shan

GREAT WALL

Baihepu
Shuiku

15 mi

15 km

0

0

The Great Wall is not a contiguous, monolithic structure. Over time, parts of the Wall have crumbled and dissolved into the sand, leaving fractured sections that begin on China's east coast and continue to the country's northwestern deserts. The Wall runs just north of Beijing, and we recommend six separate sections that you can visit easily from the capital. While there's no need to visit each section (unless you're a hiking and nature aficionado with lots of time on your hands), we think a visit to at least one is a highlight of any trip to Beijing.

❶ Badaling Great Wall. This is the Disneyland version of the wall, and the section that many Chinese aspire to visit. A trip here is convenient and quite picturesque if you don't mind the crowds. This section was constructed around 1368 of brick, stone, and soil. It was the first part to be restored, back in 1957. A cable car was built in the 1980s, which was followed by a KFC and then a Starbucks. Although it is one of the most dramatic sections of the Great Wall, the sheer number of visitors can be overwhelming. Buses leave Beijing every 5 minutes and take an hour. 🕐 *3 hr., plus 2 hr. round-trip travel time. Badaling*

Tequ, Yanqing County. ☎ *010/ 6912-2222 or 010/6912-1358. www. badaling.gov.cn. Admission ¥45. Daily 7am–6pm. Bus 919 departs from Deshengmen, every 5 min.*

❷ Huanghua Cheng. The restorations began only recently at Huanghua Cheng, which makes it a good choice if you're interested in seeing a more natural part of the Wall but don't want a hike that's too vigorous. (There's no cable car here.) The area is near a reservoir and is blanketed with yellow flowers in summer (the name Huanghua means yellow flower). The incline is gradual at first, but it gets steeper as you ascend. 🕐 *3 hr., plus 3 hr.*

The section of the Great Wall near Badaling can get extremely crowded.

The Jinshanling section of the Great Wall.

round-trip travel time. Xishuiyu, Jiuduhe Zhen, Huairou. ☎ *010/6165-1111. www.huanghuacheng.com. Admission ¥34. Mon–Fri 8am–5pm; Sat–Sun 7:30am–5:30pm.*

❸ Mutianyu. Restored in 1986, Mutianyu is slightly less crowded than Badaling. Like Badaling, it has a cable car, but Mutianyu also boasts a German-built toboggan ride, which you can take on the way down. Located in a heavily forested area, it's especially photogenic in rainy, misty weather. Public transportation for the 90-minute trip to Mutianyu is sparse, so your best bet is to rent a car for the day (p 155). ⏱ *3 hr., plus 3 hr. round-trip travel time. Mutianyu Cun, Huairou District.* ☎ *010/6162-6505. www.mutianyu greatwall.com. Admission ¥45. Daily 7:30am–5:30pm.*

❹ ★★ Jiankou. This section is for serious hikers only, and is our favorite part of the Wall. (We've spent plenty of time here, since we rent a house in the nearby countryside.) Few tourist buses make the journey here, there's no cable car, and in the off season the ticket collectors don't even bother to collect the admission fee since the area is fairly remote. You'll have to rent a car for this

excursion (p 155). Start at Xi Zha Zi Cun, where the road dead ends into a parking lot and follow the trail up to the Wall. Turn left once you reach the Wall, and prepare yourself for an intense 5-hour hike. The tallest watchtower in the distance is Jiankou; just before you reach it, look for a turnoff marked by a flat, paved section of the wall. This will lead you back down to the road. From the road, it's a 20-minute walk back to the parking lot. Make sure to bring plenty of water and a lunch. ⏱ *5 hr., plus 3 hr. round-trip travel time. Yanxi Zhen, Huairou District. No phone. Free admission officially, though nearby villagers may charge ¥5 for parking and ¥10–¥20 per person. Open 24 hr.*

❺ Jinshanling. Like Jiankou, this part of the wall is mostly unrestored, though tourist officials have installed a cable car here. Jinshanling is 10km (6¼ miles) from the Old Northern Pass, through which Qing royalty passed on the way to their summer retreat at Chengde (p 141). The Wall here, restored in the 16th century, features unusual circular towers and elaborate defensive walls leading up to towers. It is possible to do a dramatic walk from here to the Simatai section (see "Simatai," below), which takes about 5 hours. You'll have to arrange for private transportation to drop you off at Jinshanling and pick you up once you arrive in Simatai. ⏱ *3–5 hr., plus 4 hr. round-trip travel time. Bakeshiying Zhen, Luanping County, Chengde.* ☎ *0314/883-0222. www. cdchangcheng.com. Admission ¥50 (¥40 in winter). Open 7am–5pm.*

⑥ Simatai. Though the farthest from Beijing, Simatai is a good option for those who want a challenge. The most harrowing portion, steep and unrestored, is on the east (right) side of the Miyun Reservoir. The end is the Wangjing Ta, the 12th watchtower; beyond that is the Heavenly Bridge (Tianqiao) where the wall narrows to only a few feet. (Due to a series of deaths, this section is now off-limits.) The round-trip hike takes 3 hours at a moderate pace. The section of Simatai west of the reservoir leads to Jinshanling (see "Jinshanling," above). Simatai gets crowded on the weekends, especially now that a cable car has been built. On weekends, a luxury tour bus for ¥95 leaves Qianmen at 8:30am and returns to Beijing at

An unrestored section of the Great Wall at Simatai.

3pm. (Make sure to have your hotel contact the bus company to confirm the return time.) If you plan on walking to Jinshanling, it's best to arrange private transport to pick you up there. ⏱ *3–5 hr., plus 5 hr. round-trip travel time. Simatai Cun, Gubeikou Zhen, Miyun County.* ☎ *010/ 6903-1051. www.simatai-greatwall. net. Admission ¥40. Open 8am–5pm.*

A goatherder in Simatai village.

Chengde

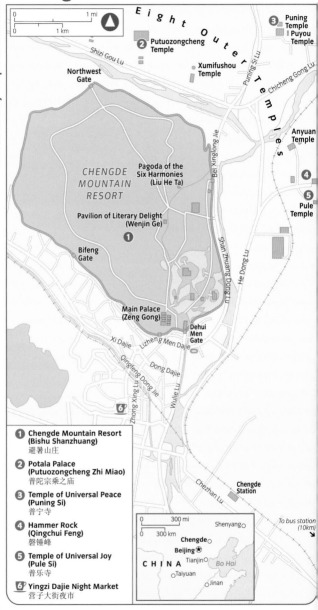

E i g h t   O u t e r   T e m p l e s

Shizi Gou Lu

Putuozongcheng Temple ❷

Xumifushou Temple

Northwest Gate

Puning Si Lu

Chicheng Gong Lu

Puning Temple ❸
Puyou Temple

Bei Xinglong Jie

CHENGDE MOUNTAIN RESORT

Pagoda of the Six Harmonies (Liu He Ta)

Anyuan Temple

Pavilion of Literary Delight (Wenjin Ge) ❶

Shan Zhuang Dong Lu

❹
Hammer Rock

❺
Pule Temple

Bifeng Gate

He Dong Lu

Main Palace (Zeng Gong)

Dehui Men Gate

Xi Dajie

Lizheng Men Dajie

Dong Dajie

Qingfeng Dong Jie

Zhong Xing Lu

Wulie Lu

❻

Chezhan Lu

Chengde Station

To bus station (10km)

❶ **Chengde Mountain Resort (Bishu Shanzhuang)**
避暑山庄

❷ **Potala Palace (Putuozongcheng Zhi Miao)**
普陀宗乘之庙

❸ **Temple of Universal Peace (Puning Si)**
普宁寺

❹ **Hammer Rock (Qingchui Feng)**
磬锤峰

❺ **Temple of Universal Joy (Pule Si)**
普乐寺

❻ **Yingzi Dajie Night Market**
营子大街夜市

0 ____ 1 mi
0 ____ 1 km

0 ____ 300 mi
0 ____ 300 km

Shenyang

Chengde
Beijing ★
Tianjin
CHINA   Bo Hai
Taiyuan
Jinan

If you can take only one overnight side trip from Beijing, go to Chengde. During the Qing dynasty, the imperial family would pack their bags and make the journey by horse in a slow procession to this summer retreat. Nowadays, a highway connects Beijing to Chengde, and the hunting grounds, pagodas, and pavilions are open to all. Make sure you focus on the old, preserved part of Chengde, which is more charming than the new city. Wandering through the parks and the temples decorated with tantric art is a relaxing change of pace if you've been in Beijing for a few days.

① ★★ Chengde Mountain Resort (Bishu Shanzhuang).

Chengde was just another village until the end of the 17th century, when the Qing emperor Kangxi stumbled upon these rolling hills near the Wuli River and decided to build this summer retreat. The first structures were commissioned in 1703. A century later, the retreat included nearly 100 imperial structures enclosed by a 9.5km-long (6-mile) wall. Until recently, emperors used these gigantic grounds dotted with lakes and pavilions for hunting, archery, and horseback riding. The park makes for an idyllic ramble, during which you can duck into several of the buildings. Not far from the Dehui Men Gate is the Main Palace (Zeng Gong), the most important of the remaining buildings. The simple, hardwood interior holds a collection of ancient military equipment, period furnishings, and antiquities. Meander along the lakes and through a rock garden to reach the Pavilion of Literary Delight (Wenjin Ge), a copy of a famous library in the southern coastal town of Ningbo. Northeast of the pavilion is the Pagoda of the Six Harmonies (Liu He Ta), a nine-story, brick structure with green-and-yellow-tiled eaves featuring bells and topped by a golden knob. ⏲ 3 hr. Lizheng Men

A view of Chengde Mountain Resort.

Dajie. ☎ 0314/216-0419. *Admission: May–Oct ¥96; Nov–Apr ¥60. 7am–6pm.*

② Potala Palace (Putuozongcheng Zhi Miao).

Modeled after Lhasa's most famous temple, this miniversion gives visitors who aren't able to go to Tibet a sense of the original. Potala Temple was built in 1771 and has more than 60 halls and terraces. It's no longer a functioning temple, but rather a museum with interesting items including statues in various sexual positions and drinking vessels made from skulls and silver. ⏱ *30 min. Shizi Guo Lu.* ☎ 0314/216-3072. *Admission ¥40 (¥30 in winter). 8am–5pm (8:30am–5pm in winter).*

③ ★ Temple of Universal Peace (Puning Si).

A 22m-high (72-ft.) copper statue of Guanyin, the goddess of mercy, stands at the center of this temple, gesturing with her 42 intricately carved arms. Climb three levels of interior galleries to look the figure in the eye. The temple, a UNESCO World Heritage Site, still attracts worshipers and contains several halls of smiling Buddhas, steles covered with Chinese characters, and red walls.

Prayer wheels at Puning Temple.

Potala Palace.

⏱ *30 min. Puning Si Lu.* ☎ 0314/205-8535. www.puningsi.com.cn. *Admission ¥50 (¥40 in winter). 7:30am–6pm (8:30am–4:30pm in winter).*

④ ★ Hammer Rock (Qingchui Feng).

Many visitors snicker when they see this natural rock formation that's shaped like a part of the male anatomy. The cable car ride to the rock offers pleasant views of the surrounding hills and fields where

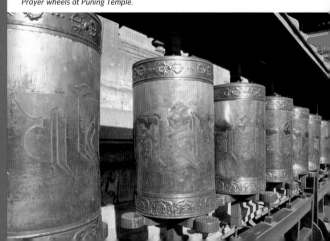

Chengde Basics

To reach Chengde, take the express train K7711, which departs from the Beijing Railway Station (☎ 010/5101-9999) at 8:07am daily and arrives at 12:29pm. You can return the next day on the express train K7712, which leaves Chengde at 1:29pm and arrives at Beijing Railway Station around 5:51pm. Buses depart regularly from Beijing's Liuliqiao Long Distance Bus Station (☎ 010/8383-1716) and arrive at the Chengde Long Distance Bus Station in 4½ hours.

We recommend staying at the **Puning Si Shangketang Dajiudian** (Puning Si; ☎ 0314/205-8544), a hotel in the Temple of Universal Peace run by monks. The cozy accommodations in the west wing of the temple are decorated with dark wood furniture and handmade paper lamps. The courtyards feature rock gardens and ponds, and the main restaurant serves vegetarian food. Late sleepers beware—the temple bells begin ringing at 7:30am. The price for a double is ¥680 to ¥10,000.

If you prefer a standard hotel, try the **Sheng Hua Dajiudian** (22 Wulie Lu; ☎ 0314/227-1188), Chengde's best hotel in terms of decor and service, with well-appointed rooms and an English-speaking staff. The price for a double is ¥780 to ¥5,000. Both hotels accept credit cards.

---

farmers harvest cabbages. ⏱ *30 min. Lamasi Cun.* ☎ *0314/205-7090. Admission ¥50. 7am–6pm.*

⑤ Temple of Universal Joy (Pule Si). Tibetan advisors helped design this temple, which was built to receive annual tributary visits from defeated Mongol tribes. The most striking element is the copy of the circular Hall of Prayer for Good Harvests from Beijing's Temple of Heaven. Shady benches around the quiet courtyard make perfect picnic spots. ⏱ *30 min. Near Hedong Lu.* ☎ *0314/205-7557. Admission ¥30. Daily 8am–5:30pm.*

⑥ Yingzi Dajie Night Market. At dusk, stalls on this central street begin selling delicious kabobs and other snacks. Yingzi Dajie. No phone. *$.*

Temple of Universal Joy.

Pingyao

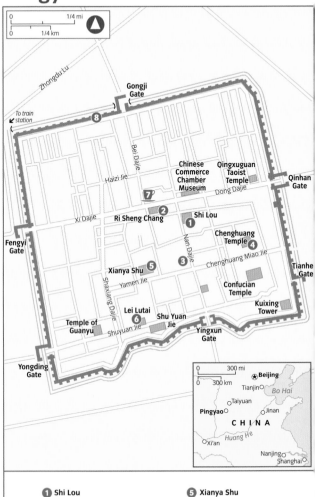

1. Shi Lou

2. Ri Sheng Chang

3. Bai Chuan Tong

4. Chenghuang Miao, Caishen Miao, & Zaojun Miao

5. Xianya Shu

6. Lei Lutai

7. Deju Yuan

8. Ancient City Wall

Tiny Pingyao is a 2,700-year-old living museum. It boasts some of the best-preserved traditional architecture in China: a Ming City wall, beautiful gray-brick courtyard homes *(siheyuan)*, extravagant family mansions, Taoist and Buddhist temples, and China's earliest commercial banks. The main drag also has some fun shops carrying antique wares. We love the street-side silversmiths making tiny slipper pendants, or abacus earrings with movable counting beads.

1 Shi Lou. Shi Lou, or Market Building, marks the center of Pingyao. Climb to the top of this three-story building to get a view of the entire city. It gets a bit crowded on the narrow landings so arrive early to avoid jostling for photo ops with the other tourists. *Free admission.*

Travel Tip

Individual entrance tickets to Pingyao's museums are not available. Instead, a 2-day pass for ¥120 gets you into the town's 20 most popular sites, including all those listed below (except Shi Lou, which is free). You can buy the pass at any of the sites or museums. Sites are

open daily from 8am to 7pm in the summer, to 6pm in the winter.

2 Ri Sheng Chang. This converted compound is the former headquarters of one of 19th-century China's leading money exchanges. It is now a museum that looks more like an elegant courtyard than a bank. It is worth having a look around the museum, which is comprised of three courtyards and almost two dozen halls and rooms. *38 Xi Dajie.* ☎ *0354/568-5364.*

3 Bai Chuan Tong. This museum exhibiting Ming and Qing furniture is housed in another of China's earliest

Shi Lou, or Market Building, in Pingyao.

Historic buildings along Nan Dajie.

banks. Displays include bedrooms, parlors, a kitchen, and a room for taking snuff (and probably opium). *109 Nan Dajie. No phone.*

④ Chenghuang Miao, Caishen Miao & Zaojun Miao. These

Gates in front of City God Taoist Temple in Pingyao's historic quarter.

three temples lie a few blocks southeast of the Market Building. They honor the city god, the god of wealth, and the kitchen god. On the north side of the courtyard is a spacious hall arranged like a court of law. An elevated altar holds a clay sculpture of the city god, with an attendant on either side. Other rows of similarly sculpted figures represent officials who attend to the god. This Ming dynasty complex burned down twice and was last rebuilt in 1864. *Chenghuang Miao Jie.* ☎ *0354/568-2250.*

⑤ Xianya Shu. This was the administrative office that meted out justice during the Ming and Qing dynasties. On the east side, there was a summoning drum. When someone had a complaint, he beat the drum to call for the Yamen chief, who would hear the case and make his judgment. Operas and reenactments of trials are performed here throughout the week. Performances are free with admission and take place Monday through Friday at 9:30, 11am, and 3:30pm; and on weekends at 9:30, 11am, 3:30, and 4:50pm. *Chenghuang Miao Jie (head west of the temples until the road becomes Zhengfujie).* ☎ *0354/568-2909.*

6 Lei Lutai. The former home of pioneering banker Lei Lutai (1770–1849) is a fine example of a wealthy urban residence. It has four rows of connecting courtyards, each done in a different style. *Shuyuan Jie.* ☎ *0354/562-7660.*

7 Deju Yuan. This guesthouse has not only excellent cooking, but also a gracious host. An order of Shanxi specialty laolao you mian (small rings of husked oat pasta served pressed together in a bamboo steamer) is a perfect snack for two in the middle of the afternoon. *43 Xi Dajie.* ☎ *0354/568-5266. $.*

8 ★ kids Ancient City Wall. This 6.4km-long (4-mile) city wall is ideal for walking and taking in the

A traditional residence house in Pingyao.

The city of Pingyao.

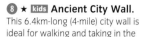

Pingyao's ancient city wall.

breathtaking view of Pingyao's courtyard rooftops and the outlying areas. It is a well-preserved Ming dynasty wall made of rammed earth and bricks. At dusk, locals often come up here to rehearse dance steps and kids horse around playing Chinese hacky sack. ●

Pingyao Basics

Take the number 1163 or K603 overnight train from Beijing West station to arrive in Pingyao in the morning. If you can, reserve a seat on train 1163. It pulls into Pingyao at 7:31am, allowing you to sleep slightly longer than train K603, which arrives at 5:33am.

During the day, taxis are not allowed within the old city wall, which is where you will want to spend your time. The only time you need to take a taxi is to and from the railway station. Both of the hotels recommended in this tour offer free taxi transfers for people arriving on the morning train. You'll be taken from the station to the nearest city gate. From there, the hotel staff will guide you to the hotel.

For hotels, we recommend ★★ **Deju Yuan** (43 Xi Dajie; ☎ 0354/568-5266). Standard rooms come with large kang beds (heated brick beds). A three-bedroom suite has two bedrooms connected by a living room and is ideal for families. They also have Internet access. Another excellent courtyard guesthouse is **Tian Yuan Kui** (73 Nan Dajie; ☎ 0354/568-0069). The service and amenities are similar to those at Deju Yuan, with the added bonus of a sauna.

The
Savvy Traveler

Before You Go

Government Tourist Offices

In the **United States:** 350 Fifth Ave., Ste. 6413, Empire State Building, New York, NY 10118 (☎ **212/760-8218**, 760-8807, or 760-4002; fax 212/760-8809; ny@cnta.gov.cn); 600 W. Broadway, Ste. 320, Glendale, CA 91204 (☎ **818/545-7505;** fax 828/545-7506; la@cnta.gov.cn). In **Canada:** 480 University Ave., Suite 806, Toronto, ONT M5G 1V2 (☎ **416/599-6636;** fax 416/599-6382; www.tourismchina-ca.com). In the **U.K.:** 71 Warwick Rd., London SW5 9HB (☎ **020/7373-0888;** fax 020/7370-9989; london@cnta.gov.cn). In **Australia:** Level 19, 44 Market St., Sydney, NSW 2000 (☎ **020/9299-4057;** fax 020/9290-1958; sydney@cnta.gov.cn).

The Best Times to Go

Fall is the ideal time to visit. September and October have plenty of warm, dry, sunny days with clear skies and perfectly cool evenings. The next best time is March through May, when winds blow away the pollution but also sometimes bring sandstorms for a day or two, turning the sky yellow and leaving a film of dust behind. Winters are usually cold and very dry; summer is hot and humid.

Festivals & Special Events

WINTER. **Chinese New Year** (Spring Festival) operates on the lunar calendar. Solar equivalents for the next few years are February 3, 2011; January 23, 2012; February 10, 2013; and January 31, 2014. The effects of this holiday are felt 2 weeks before the date and 2 weeks after. The most spectacular event happens on New Year's Eve at midnight, when the entire city sets off fireworks and the sky is awash in exploding colors for an hour or two. There are also several temple fairs around town with games, shows, and vendors selling traditional toys and snacks. The best ones are at Ditan Park (A2 Andingmenwai Dajie; ☎ 010/6421-4657), and Chaoyang Park (1 Nongzhanguan Nanlu; ☎ 010/6506-7723).

SPRING. In addition to the national holiday May 1, celebrating International Worker's Day (Labor Day), China has recently created two lunar calendar holidays: Tomb Sweeping Day and Dragon Boat Festival, official holidays. Tomb Sweeping Day usually falls sometime in April, while Dragon Boat Festival is sometime in May or June. The **Midi Festival** takes place around May 1 over a weekend and features punk, rock, and experimental music in Haidian Park. See www.midifestival.com for more information.

SUMMER. Summer is a quiet time for festivals and holidays. Most universities take a 2-month break in July and August.

FALL. The most important holiday of the fall is Mid-Autumn Moon Festival, which marks the beginning of harvest time across China. Chinese celebrate the holiday on the 15th day of the 8th lunar month, by gazing at the full moon and eating sweet, or occasionally savory, pastries called mooncakes. The holiday usually falls in September or early October. A second important holiday is October 1, marking the founding of the People's Republic of China in 1949. In September, you can catch local and international pop and rock bands during the **Beijing**

Previous page: Bikers in Beijing.

BEIJING'S AVERAGE TEMPERATURES & RAINFALL						
	JAN	FEB	MAR	APR	MAY	JUNE
Temp. (°F)	26	31	43	57	68	76
Temp. (°C)	−3	−1	6	14	20	24
Days of Rain	2.1	3.1	4.5	5.1	6.4	9.7
	JULY	AUG	SEPT	OCT	NOV	DEC
Temp. (°F)	79	77	69	57	41	30
Temp. (°C)	26	25	21	14	5	−1
Days of Rain	14.5	14.1	6.9	5.0	3.6	1.6

Pop Festival (www.beijingpop festival.com), an outdoor festival held in Chaoyang Park. The **China Open** (www.chinaopen.cn) usually takes place in mid-September. The event draws numerous international tennis stars, and has grown in popularity now that Chinese players are holding their own in the international arena. The **Beijing Music Festival** celebrates classical music, luring international orchestras and guest performers to the nation's capital in mid-October (www.bmf. org.cn).

The Weather

Siberian air masses that move south across the Mongolian plateau bring cold, dry winters to Beijing. Monsoon winds from the southeast mean summers are extremely hot and humid. Spring and fall are the shortest seasons in Beijing and the best times to visit, specifically April and May and September and October. For daily weather forecasts, check *China Daily* or CCTV 9, China Central Television's English channel (broadcast in most hotels).

Useful Websites

- **www.ebeijing.gov.cn**: This official Beijing government website provides information on travel and news in Beijing.
- **www.chinesepod.com**: Here you can download podcasts of elementary, intermediate, and advanced Chinese-language lessons.
- **http://ditu.google.cn**: If you can type Chinese characters (or copy and paste from another document), this interactive map of Beijing and China is invaluable.
- **www.thatsbj.com**: This is the best place to find up-to-date information on arts and entertainment events around town.
- **www.time-blog.com/china_ blog**: *Time* magazine's blog serves bite-size portions of the latest newsworthy events in China.
- **www.timeout.com/travel/ beijing**: *Time Out* provides a brief overview of the city.
- **www.weather.com**: Up-to-the-minute worldwide weather reports.

Internet Access in China

The internet is monitored in China and websites that mention Tibet, Falun Gong, and the Tian'anmen Massacre are frequently blocked. Facebook and certain news sites like BBC are also frequently inaccessible in China. To circumvent the firewall, you may want to suscribe to a VPN before you arrive in China. One highly recommended service is Witopia (www.witopia.net).

Cellphones (Mobile Phones)

Beijing (and all of China) is on the GSM tri-band network, so make sure the cellphone you bring is compatible. You may need to have your service provider "unlock" your cellphone to use it with a local provider. The cheap and painless way to get talking is to buy a SIM card at a cellphone shop. A popular provider is China Mobile; it charges ¥0.60 per minute. Add money to your card with prepaid calling cards that range from ¥50 to ¥100 and are available at kiosks around town.

Visa Requirements

All visitors to mainland China must obtain a visa in advance. Visa applications typically take 3 to 5 working days to process, although this can be shortened to as little as 1 day if you apply in person and pay extra fees. "L" (tourist) visas are valid for between 1 and 3 months. Usually 1 month is granted unless you request more, which you may or may not get according to events in China at the time. Double-entry tourist visas are also available. It varies, but typically your visit must *begin* within 90 days of the date of issue.

Getting **There**

By Plane

China's international airlines often offer lower rates than foreign carriers for direct, nonstop flights. Many of them have partnerships with international airlines, so you can still cash in on those coveted frequent-flyer miles. Air China is one of the better airlines. They have recently joined international aviation network Star Alliance, and are currently partners with United. Only one major airport, Beijing Capital International airport (PEK), serves Beijing. For a list of airlines that fly to Beijing, see p 176.

Getting to & from the airport: You will be pestered by **taxi** touts as soon as you emerge from customs. *Never* go with these people. Instead, head to the taxi queue straight ahead. Rates are ¥10 for the first 2km (1 mile) and ¥2 for each additional kilometer. The meter starts at ¥11 after 11pm. From PEK, the approximate fare is ¥64 to ¥96 for a 20- to 30-minute trip, including the ¥10 highway toll.

Airport shuttle buses (☎ 010/6459-4375 or -4376; www.bcia.com.cn/en/passengers_Land_airport_page.html) depart from just outside the international arrivals area. There are six different routes that connect to several major areas around town. Destinations include San Yuan Qiao (near the Hilton and Sheraton hotels), the Dong Zhi Men and Dong Si Shi Tiao subway stations, the Beijing Railway Station, and Hangtian Qiao (near the Marriot West). The fee is ¥16, regardless of your destination or stop.

By Train

From Hung Hom station in Kowloon (Hong Kong), expresses run directly to Beijing West Station on alternate days; go to www.kcrc.com for schedules and fares. From Moscow there are weekly trains via Ulaan Baatar in Mongolia to Beijing, and weekly via a more easterly route directly to Harbin in China's northeast and down to the capital. There's also a separate weekly run from Ulaan Baatar to Beijing. Trains run twice weekly from Hanoi in Vietnam to Beijing West via Guilin. There's also a service between Beijing and Pyongyang in North Korea, but you'll only be on that if you've joined an organized tour.

Etiquette & Customs

Wear whatever you find comfortable. Some of the diaphanous or apparently sprayed-on clothing of younger Chinese women is more likely to surprise you than your attire will surprise them. Foreigners are stared at regardless of what they wear. Swimwear should tend toward the conservative by Western standards—swimsuits rather than bikinis for women—but not if you are using pools in deluxe hotels with foreign guests. Business attire is similar to that of the West. For most visitors, opportunities to dress up formally are few; no restaurants or hotels absolutely require a jacket or tie for men.

Greetings and gestures: The handshake is now used as it is in the West, although there's a tendency to hang on longer. Bring business cards if you have them, as an exchange of cards almost always follows a greeting. Present yours with two hands, and then hold the one you're given with two hands. If you can speak even two words of Mandarin, you will be told that you speak very well. This is something you should deny even if you are fluent.

Avoiding offense: However great the provocation, do not lose your temper and shout at someone in public or cause him or her to experience public shame (loss of face). Even flatly contradicting someone in front of others (so he loses face) is also best avoided if harmony is to be maintained. Instead, complain calmly and privately, and directly to a superior if you wish. Punctuality is very important in China, and the traffic situation in most cities makes that difficult, so allow plenty of time to get where you are going if you are meeting someone.

Eating and drinking: Master the use of chopsticks before you go. Suggestions made by the host that the food is lacking in some way should always be greeted with firm denials. Serve yourself from main dishes using the spoon provided, then eat with chopsticks. Do not leave them sticking up out of your bowl. Your cup of tea will constantly be topped off—if you don't want any more, leave it full. There's a great deal of competitive drinking at banquets, which is done by the simultaneous drinking of toasts in bai jiu (Chinese spirits), to cries of "Gan bei!" ("dry cup"—down in one). Avoid participation by drinking beer or mineral water instead, but if toasts of welcome are made, be sure to make one in reply. Dining tends to happen early, and at the end of the meal everyone disappears quickly. If you are invited to eat at someone's home, be sure to take off your shoes at the entrance (your host's protestations that it's not necessary are merely polite).

Getting **Around**

By Taxi

Taxis are everywhere and are a convenient way to travel around town if you avoid rush hour. Fares are ¥10 for the first 2km (1 mile) and ¥2 for each additional kilometer. The meter starts at ¥11 after 11pm.

By Subway (ditie)

Beijing has massively expanded its subway lines over the last 5 years. At press time, eight subway lines were open and most destinations within the center of town are reachable via subway and a 5- to 10-minute walk. Fares for paper tickets are ¥3 to ¥5. Alternatively, you can buy an electronic card that can be used for subway and bus rides. The subway card, officially known as the "Municipal Administration and Communication Card" (Shizheng Jiaotong Yikatong) can be bought for a ¥40 minimum (including ¥20 for deposit). Throughout this guide, note that if a destination is a 5- to 10-minute walk from a subway stop, we've included the name of the subway stop at the end of the entry. If no subway stop is listed, your best bet is to take a taxi.

By Bus

Beijing buses can be slightly daunting. Rush hour is particularly painful, as people are jammed into them like sardines in a can. But if you can navigate your way to your final destination, you'll spend very little. Fares range from ¥1 to ¥5. Subway cards (see "By Subway," above) get you 20% to 60% fare discounts, making the journey even more affordable.

By Bike

Beijing is flat, so biking is an excellent means of travel. See "Bike Rentals" in "Fast Facts," below. Whenever possible, try to park the bike in marked and supervised enclosures, using the lock, or expect the bike to be gone when you get back. The parking fee is usually ¥0.20.

Fast **Facts**

APARTMENT RENTALS Check out http://beijing.craigslist.org and www.homtel.cn/e/eindex.asp for short-term housing needs. You'll likely negotiate a rental directly from the unit's owner.

ATMS/CASHPOINTS As in most cities these days, obtaining money is a simple matter of lining up at the nearest ATM and plugging in your bank card. Visa ATM Locator (www.visa.com) gives locations of PLUS ATMs worldwide; MasterCard ATM Locator (www.mastercard.com) provides locations of Cirrus ATMs worldwide.

BANKING HOURS Most banks are open Monday through Friday 9am to 5:30pm, Saturday and Sunday 10am to 5pm. Many banks also have ATMs for 24-hour banking.

BIKE RENTALS If you want to bike around Tian'anmen, your best bet is Cycle China (12 Jingshan Dong Lu; ☎ 010/6402-5653 or 0/139-1188-6524). Rental prices are ¥60 to ¥80 per day (including helmets and locks), and the deposit is ¥400.

BUSINESS HOURS Offices are generally open 9am to 6pm, but closed Saturday and Sunday. All shops,

What Things Cost in Beijing

	Yuan ¥	U.S. $	U.K. £
Taxi from airport to city center	75.00–	9.75–	4.90–
plus ¥10 toll fee (use meter!)	100.00	13.00	6.50
Up to 3km (less than 2miles) by taxi	10.00	1.30	0.65
Metro ride	3.00	0.38	0.20
Local telephone call	0.50	0.07	0.03
Hearty bowl of beef noodles at a basic restaurant	4.80	0.60	0.32
Regular coffee at Starbucks	12.00	1.50	0.81
McDonald's set meal for one	18.00	2.25	1.21
Dinner for two at a simple homestyle restaurant	30.00	3.75	2.02
Dinner for two in foreigner-frequented areas	150.00	19.50	9.75
Dinner for two in top hotel restaurant	640.00	80.00	43.00
Bottle of beer at an ordinary restaurant or store	3.00	0.38	0.20
Bottle of beer in a foreigner-frequented bar district	30.00	3.80	2.04
Admission to the Forbidden City	60.00	7.50	4.32
Admission to the Lama Temple	25.00	3.35	1.63

sights, restaurants, and transport systems offer the same service 7 days a week. Shops are typically open at least 8am to 8pm.

CAR RENTALS Because of the many driving hazards in Beijing, renting a car is not recommended for visitors. Taking taxis is cheaper and easier. If you must, Hertz (www.hertz.net.cn) has offices at 205 Ocean International Center, Tower A, Dong Sihuan Zhong Lu (☎ 010/5908-1313), open 9am to 6pm weekdays. The big snag is that a Chinese driver's license and a residence permit are required, something no short-term visitor will be able to arrange, but you can rent a car with a driver. The fleet is fairly battered (locals rent cars when learning to drive), and it's often difficult to obtain a vehicle on weekends.

CLIMATE See "The Weather," above.

CONCERTS See "Tickets," later in this chapter.

CREDIT CARDS Credit cards are becoming a more convenient method of payment in Beijing, though you should carry some cash with you as well, especially for shopping trips. Most places are cash only and those that accept credit cards often charge an additional fee, anywhere from 2% to 4%.

CURRENCY Larger branches of the Bank of China typically exchange cash and traveler's checks on weekdays only, from 9am to 4pm, occasionally with a break for lunch (11:30am–1:30pm). Most central is the branch at the bottom of Wangfujing Dajie, next to the Oriental Plaza. Other useful branches include those at Fucheng Men Nei Dajie 410; on Jianguo Men Wai Dajie, west of the Scitech Building; in the Lufthansa Center, next to the Kempinski Hotel; and in Tower 1 of the China World Trade Center. You will need to bring your passport. See "Money," p 158.

CUSTOMS Fill out all the forms that the flight attendants hand out on the plane. Forgetting one will send you all the way to the back of the line at the airport and it can be incredibly frustrating. At press time, most international travelers must fill out a Quarantine Form, an Entry Form, and a Customs Form.

DENTISTS The reputable services are **Arrail** (208 CITIC Bldg., 19 Jianguomenwai Dajie; ☎ 010/6500-6473; www.arrail-dental.com; appointments need to be made 2 days in advance), and **King's Dental** (Shop 118, G/F Beijing Towercrest Plaza no. 3 Maizidian Xilu; ☎ 010/8458-0388; www.kings dental.com).

DINING Dining in Beijing is extremely casual and jackets for men are rarely required. Reservations are also not a concern, except for some popular places such as Maison Boulud (p 81) and Made in China (p 81).

DOCTORS The SOS International Clinic (105 Kunsha Bldg., 16 Xinyuanli, Chaoyang District; ☎ 010/6462-9112) and Beijing United Family Hospital (2 Jiang Tai Lu, Chao Yang District; ☎ 010/5927-7000) reputedly offer excellent and comprehensive care in many languages.

ELECTRICITY The electric voltage in Beijing is 220V/50Hz and the standard wall socket has three connectors. Most electrical devices from North America, therefore, cannot be

used without a transformer. Some outlets take the North American two-flat-pin plug (but not the three-pin version, or those with one pin broader than the other). Nearly as common are outlets for the two-round-pin plugs common in Europe. Outlets for the three-flat-pin (two pins at an angle) used in Australia, for instance, are also frequently seen. Most hotel rooms have all three, and indeed many outlets are designed to take all three plugs.

EMBASSIES Beijing has two main embassy areas—one surrounding Ritan Gongyuan, north of Jianguo Men Wai Dajie, and another in San Li Tun, north of Gongti Bei Lu. A third district, future home of the new U.S. Embassy, has sprouted up next to the Hilton Hotel outside the north section of East Third Ring Road. Embassies are typically open Monday through Friday from 9am to 4 or 5pm, with a lunch break from noon to 1:30pm. The U.S. Embassy is at 55 An Jia Lou Lu, north of Liangmahe Lu near the Luftansa Center (☎ 010/8531-4000). The Canadian Embassy is at Dong Zhi Men Wai Dajie 19 (☎ 010/5139-4449). The British Embassy consular section is in Ritan at Floor 21, North Tower, Kerry Centre, 1 Guanghua Lu (☎ 010/5192-4239). The Australian Embassy is in San Li Tun at 21 Dong Zhi Men Wai Dajie (☎ 010/5140-4111). The New Zealand Embassy is in Ritan at 1 Dong Er Jie (☎ 010/6532-7000).

EMERGENCIES Dial ☎ 120 for emergency medical services; dial ☎ 110 for all other emergencies.

EVENT LISTINGS Your best bets online are City Weekend (www.city weekend.com.cn/beijing) and The Beijinger (www.thebeijinger.com) for restaurant, bar, and upcoming event listings. In Beijing, look for *Time Out Beijing* and *The Beijinger*, two monthly magazines, for up-to-date listings.

HOLIDAYS Banks, government offices, post offices, and many stores, restaurants, and museums are closed on the following national holidays: New Year's Day (Jan 1), Spring Festival (Chinese New Year's day and the following 2 days—see "Festivals & Special Events," earlier in this chapter for exact dates in coming years), Tomb Sweeping Day (a lunar holiday sometime in Apr), Labor Day (May 1), Dragon Boat Festival (a lunar holiday usually celebrated in May or June), Mid-Autumn Moon Festival (a lunar holiday in Sept or Oct), and National Day (Oct 1).

INSURANCE Check your existing insurance policies and credit card coverage before you buy travel insurance. You may already be covered for lost luggage, canceled tickets, or medical expenses. The cost of travel insurance varies widely, depending on the cost and length of your trip, your age, your health, and the type of trip you're taking.

Trip-cancellation insurance helps you get your money back if you have to back out of a trip, if you have to go home early, or if your travel supplier goes bankrupt. Allowable reasons for cancellation can range from sickness to natural disasters to a government department declaring your destination unsafe for travel. Insurers usually won't cover vague fears, though.

For China, purchase **medical insurance** that includes an air ambulance or scheduled airline repatriation. Be clear on the terms and conditions—is repatriation limited to life-threatening illnesses, for instance? While there are advanced facilities staffed by foreign doctors in Beijing, regular Chinese hospitals are to be avoided. They may charge you a substantial bill, which you must pay in cash before you're allowed to leave. If this happens to you, you'll have to wait until you return home to submit your claim, so make sure you have adequate proof of payment.

Lost-luggage insurance: On U.S. domestic flights, checked baggage is covered up to $2,800 per ticketed passenger. On international flights (including U.S. portions of international trips), baggage is limited to approximately $9.07 per pound, up to approximately $635 per checked bag. If you plan to check items more valuable than the standard liability, see if your valuables are covered by your homeowner's policy, or get baggage insurance as part of your comprehensive travel-insurance package. Read the policy carefully—some valuables are effectively uninsurable, and others have such high excess charges that the insurance is not worth buying.

If your luggage is lost, immediately file a lost-luggage claim at the airport. For most airlines, you must report delayed, damaged, or lost baggage within 4 hours of arrival. The airlines are required to deliver luggage, once found, directly to your house or destination free of charge, although don't expect that necessarily to work with domestic Chinese airlines.

INTERNET Beijing has many Wi-Fi locations at restaurants, cafes, and hotels and Internet cafes are popular among youth. Web surfing may be monitored and access to websites deemed sensitive by the government is often denied. If the request is for a site that is on the government's blacklist (Wikipedia, at the time of this writing, for example), it won't get through. If you want to surf the Web on your personal computer without running into such problems, consider signing up for a Web proxy service such as Witopia (www.witopia.net) before you arrive in China.

LOST PROPERTY Be sure to contact all of your credit card companies the minute you discover your wallet has been lost or stolen. Your credit card company or insurer may require a police report number or record of the loss, although many Public Security Bureaus (police stations) will be reluctant to do anything as energetic as lift a pen. Most credit card companies have an emergency toll-free number to call if your card is lost or stolen: In mainland China, **Visa**'s emergency number is ☎ 800/711-2911 or 800/110-2911; **American Express** cardholders and traveler's check holders should call ☎ 010/800-610-0277; **MasterCard** holders should call ☎ 800/722-7111. For lost passports, contact your embassy or consulate and proceed to the main Public Security Bureau (see "Police," below).

MAIL & POSTAGE Sending mail from China is cheap and remarkably reliable. Letters and cards written in red ink will occasionally be rejected, as this carries extremely negative overtones. Costs are as follows: **postcards ¥4.20, letters under 10 grams ¥5.40, letters under 20 grams ¥6.50. EMS** is an international express delivery service for letters and parcels—prices vary by weight.

MONEY The word *yuan* (¥) is rarely spoken, nor is *jiao,* the written form for one-tenth of a *yuan,* equivalent to 10 *fen* (there are 100 *fen* in a *yuan*). Instead, the Chinese speak of "pieces of money," *kuai qian,* usually abbreviated just to *kuai;* and they speak of *mao* for one-tenth of a *kuai. Fen* have been overtaken by inflation and are almost useless. Often all zeros after the last whole number are simply omitted, along with *kuai qian,* which is taken as read, especially in direct reply to the question *duoshao qian*— "How much?"

PASSPORT Visitors must have a valid passport with at least 6 months' validity and two blank pages remaining (you *may* get away with just one blank page).

PHARMACIES **Golden Elephant** (277 Wangfujing Dajie; ☎ 010/6522-9135) is a reputable pharmacy chain where you'll find a stock of familiar drugs (hooray for Tylenol). Branches of Watson's are also a good bet (on the first floor of Full Link Plaza at Chaoyang Men Wai Dajie 19, and in the basement of the Oriental Plaza at the bottom of Wangfujing Dajie 1; 10am–9pm). They stock most common remedies and toiletries, mostly in the British versions. For more specific drugs, try the pharmacy in the **Beijing United Family Hospital** or the **SOS Clinic** (see "Doctors," above).

POLICE The police (*jingcha*) are quite simply best avoided—honestly, many are keen to avoid doing any work. Ideally, any interaction with the police should be limited to visa extensions. If you must see them for some reason, approach your hotel for assistance first, and visit the main Public Security Bureau (*gong'an ju* in Chinese, "PSB") to foreigners) office on the south side of the eastern North Second Ring Road, just east of the Lama Temple subway stop (☎ 010/8401-5300; Mon–Sat 8:30am–4:30pm).

POST OFFICE There are numerous **China Post** offices around the city, including one inside the Landmark Hotel (next to the Great Wall Sheraton), one on Di'anmenwai Dajie (1 block south of the Drum Tower), the main office on Jianguomenwai Dajie (almost opposite the

International Hotel), and the **EMS Post Office** (Beijing Youzheng Sudi Ju) at the corner of Qianmen Dong Dajie and Zhengyi Lu. There is a **FedEx** office in Oriental Plaza, room 107, number 1 Office Building. **DHL** has branches in the China World Center and COFCO Plaza.

SAFETY   China is one of Asia's safest destinations. As anywhere else, though, you should be cautious of theft in places such as crowded markets, popular tourist sites, bus and railway stations, and airports.

SMOKING   Given the city's pollution levels, the generally lax attitude to public smoking should come as no surprise. Nonsmoking tables in restaurants are pretty much nonexistent. Smokers are usually sent to the spaces between carriages on trains, and buses are usually smoke-free havens.

STAYING HEALTHY   The greatest risk to the enjoyment of a vacation in China is one of stomach upsets or more serious illnesses arising from low hygiene standards. Keep your hands frequently washed and away from your mouth. Only eat freshly cooked hot food, and fruit you can peel yourself—avoid touching the part to be eaten once it's been peeled. Drink only boiled or bottled water. *Never* drink from the tap. Use bottled water for brushing your teeth.

TAXIS   See "Getting Around," earlier in this chapter.

TELEPHONES   The international country code for mainland China is 86. **To call China:** Dial the international access code (011 in the U.S., 00 in the U.K., for example), then the country code (86 for China), then the city code, omitting the initial zero, and then the number. To reach Beijing from North America, you would dial 011-86-10-plus the

eight-digit number. From the U.K., you would dial 00-86-10 plus the eight-digit number. **To call within China:** For calls within the same city, omit the city code, which always begins with a zero (010 for Beijing, 020 for Guangzhou, for example). All hotel phones have direct dialing, and most have international dialing. Hotels are only allowed to add a service charge of up to 15% to the cost of the call, and even long-distance rates within China are very low. To use a public telephone, you'll need an IC (integrated circuit) card, available from post offices, convenience stores, and street stalls. IC cards are available in values beginning at ¥20 (you can purchase these wherever you can make out the letters "IC" among the Chinese characters). A brief local call is typically ¥0.30 to ¥0.50. Phones show you the value remaining on the card when you insert it, and count down as you talk.

To make international calls: First dial 00 and then the country code (1 for the U.S. or Canada, 44 for the U.K., 353 for Ireland, 61 for Australia, 64 for New Zealand). Next dial the area or city code, omitting any leading zero, and then dial the number. For example, if you want to call the British Embassy in Washington, D.C., you would dial 00-1-202-588-7800. Forget taking access numbers for your local phone company with you—you can call internationally for a fraction of the cost by using an IP (Internet protocol) card, available wherever you see the letters "IP." You should bargain to pay less than the face value of the card—as little as ¥40 for a ¥100 card from street vendors. Instructions for use are on the back, but you simply dial the access number given, choose English from the menu, and follow the instructions to dial in the number behind a scratch-off panel. Depending on where you call, ¥50 can give you an hour of talking. If using a public phone, you'll need an IC card to make the call. In emergencies, dial ☎108 to negotiate a collect call, but you'll need help from a Mandarin speaker.

For directory assistance: Dial ☎ 114. No English is spoken, and only local numbers are available. If you want numbers for other cities, dial the city code followed by 114—a long-distance call. You can text the name of the establishment you are looking for (in English) to 85880, and for a small fee, the address will return in Chinese, ready to show to your taxi driver.

For operator assistance: Just ask for help at your hotel.

Toll-free numbers: Numbers beginning with 800 within China are toll-free, but calling a 1-800 number in the States from China is a full-tariff international call, as is calling one in Hong Kong from mainland China, or vice versa.

TICKETS   A reliable online box office is **Piao** (www.piao.com.cn or ☎ 400/610-3721). They sell tickets to the latest musical, dance, and sports events. You can visit them at 7F, 32 Dongzhong Jie.

TIME ZONE   All of China is on Beijing time—8 hours ahead of GMT (and therefore of London), 13 hours ahead of New York, 14 hours ahead of Chicago, and 16 hours ahead of Los Angeles. There's no daylight saving time.

TIPPING   In mainland China there is generally no tipping. Until recently, tipping was expressly forbidden, and some hotels still carry signs requesting you not to tip. Foreigners, especially those on tours, are overcharged at every turn, and it bemuses Chinese that they hand out free money in addition. Chinese never do it themselves, and indeed if a bellhop or other hotel employee hints that a tip would be welcome, he or she is likely to be fired. Waitresses may run out of restaurants after you to return a tip to you, and all but the most corrupt of taxi drivers will insist on returning a tip, too. Hotel employees and taxi drivers are already far better paid than the average Chinese, and to be a tour guide is already a license to print money. In China, the listed price or the price bargained for is the price you pay, and that's that.

TOILETS   Many are now staffed by service attendants and have been upgraded from open dirt pits to porcelain squatter toilets in separate stalls (with doors!). Free soap and toilet paper, however, is expecting too much. Travel with your own tissues and wet naps.

Beijing: A Brief History

930–1122 A provincial town roughly on the site of modern Beijing becomes the southern capital of the Khitan Mongol Liao dynasty.

1122–1215 The city is taken over by the Jurchen Tartar Jin dynasty.

1215 Mongol emperor Genghis Khan descends into the capital and razes everything in sight.

1267–93 Under Kublai Khan's (Genghis' grandson) rule, the capital Khanbalik (Khan's town) is constructed. It's known as Da Du (Great Capital) in Mandarin; Cambulac in Marco Polo's account of the city.

1271 Kublai Khan formally adopts the new dynasty's name: the

Yuan (1215–1368). By 1279, Kublai Khan makes himself ruler of the largest empire the world has ever known.

1273–92 Marco Polo's ghostwritten account of his time in Khanbalik captures the imagination of European readers.

1368 The Ming dynasty, having driven out the Mongols, establishes its capital at Nanjing. Da Du becomes Beiping (The Pacified North).

1420 The Yongle emperor becomes the first Chinese emperor to reign from Beijing. The Forbidden City and Temple of Heaven are constructed.

1550 In response to Mongol attacks, a lower southern extension to the city wall is begun, eventually enclosing the commercial district, the important ceremonial sites of the Temple (Altar) of Heaven and Altar of Agriculture, and a broad swath of countryside (which remains free of buildings well into the 20th c.). Beijing remains largely the same for the next 400 years.

1644–1911 As peasant rebels overrun the capital, the last Ming emperor is driven to suicide. Shortly afterward, the rebels are driven out by invading Manchu forces, whose Qing dynasty transfers its capital from Manchuria to Beijing, absorbing China into its own empire. Chinese are expelled from the northern section of the city, which becomes the home of Manchu military and courtiers. The southern section becomes the Chinese quarter of Beijing.

1793–94 George III's emissary to the Qianlong emperor visits China and passes through Beijing, staying outside the city in a vast area of parks and palaces. His requests for increased trade and for a permanent trade representative in Beijing are turned down. When the Qianlong emperor dies in 1799, the government is terminally corrupt and in decline.

1858 The Second Opium War sees the Qing and their Chinese subjects capitulating in the face of the superior military technology of "barbarians" (principally the British) for the second time in 16 years. Under the terms of the Treaty of Nanjing, China is forced to permit the permanent residence of foreign diplomats and trade representatives in the capital.

1860 The Qing imprison and murder foreign representatives sent for the treaty's ratification. British and French rescue forces occupy Beijing and destroy a vast area of parks and palaces to the northwest. Foreign powers begin to construct diplomatic legation buildings just inside the Tartar City's wall east of Qian Men.

1900 The Harmonious Fists, nicknamed the Boxers, a superstitious, antiforeign peasant movement, besieges the foreign residents of the Legation Quarter, with the initially covert and finally open assistance of imperial troops. The siege begins on June 19 and is only lifted, after extensive destruction and many deaths, by the forces of Eight Allied Powers (several European nations, Japan, and the United States) on August 14. Boxers, imperial troops, Chinese, foreign survivors, and allied soldiers take to looting the city. Payments on a vast indemnity take the Qing a further 39 years to pay in full, although the British and Americans use much of the income to help found Yan-ching (now Peking) University and other institutions, and to pay for young Chinese to study overseas.

1911 The Qing dynasty's downfall is brought about by an almost accidental revolution, and betrayal by Yuan Shikai, the man the Qing trusted to crush it. He negotiates with both sides and extracts an abdication agreement from the regent of the infant emperor, Puyi, and an agreement from the rebels that he will become the first president of the new republic.

1915 Yuan Shikai revives annual ceremonies at the Temple of Heaven, and prepares to install himself as the first emperor of a new dynasty, but widespread demonstrations and the fomenting of a new rebellion in the south lead him to cancel his plans. He dies the following year.

1917 In July a promonarchist warlord puts Puyi back on the throne, but he is driven out by another warlord who drops three bombs on the Forbidden City.

1919 Students and citizens gather on May 4 in Tian'anmen Square to protest the government's agreement that Chinese territory formerly under German control be handed to the Japanese.

1924 The Qing emperor is removed by a hostile warlord and put under house arrest, later escaping to the Legation Quarter with the help of his Scottish former tutor.

1928 Nationalist Party forces in the south declare Nanjing the capital, and Beijing reverts to the name of Beiping. In the following years many ancient buildings are vandalized or covered in political slogans.

1933 With Japanese armies seemingly poised to occupy Beiping, the most important pieces of the imperial collection of antiquities in the Forbidden City are packed into 19,557 crates and moved to Shanghai. They move again when the Japanese take Shanghai in 1937, and eventually 13,484 crates end up with the Nationalist government in Taiwan in 1949.

1937 Japanese forces occupy Beijing, and stay until the end of World War II.

1949 Mao Zedong proclaims the creation of the People's Republic of China. A vast flood of refugees from the countryside takes over the courtyard houses commandeered from their owners. Temples are turned into army barracks, storehouses, and light industrial units.

1950 The Chinese army defeats the Tibetan army and claims sovereignty over the region.

1958–59 In a series of major projects to mark 10 years of Communist rule, the old ministries lining what will be Tian'anmen Square and its surrounding walls are flattened for the construction of the Great Hall of the People and the vast museums opposite. These and Beijing Railway Station are built with Soviet help. The 400-year-old city walls are pulled down and replaced with a subway line and a ring road.

1966–76 The destruction reaches its peak as bands of Red Guards ransack ancient buildings, burn books, and smash art. Intellectuals are bullied, imprisoned, tortured, and murdered, as are many with a history of links to foreigners. Scores are settled, and millions die. The education system largely comes to a halt. Many antiquities impounded from their owners are sold to foreign dealers by weight to provide funds for the government, which later decries foreign theft of Chinese antiquities.

1972 President Richard Nixon arrives in Beijing for a 7-day stay. The visit marks a turning point in relations between the U.S. and China.

1976 The death of Zhou Enlai, who is credited with mitigating some of the worst excesses of the Cultural Revolution, motivates more than 100,000 people to demonstrate against the government in Tian'anmen Square. The demonstrations are labeled counterrevolutionary, and hundreds are arrested. The death of Mao Zedong, himself thought to be responsible for an estimated 38 million deaths, effectively brings the Cultural Revolution to an end. Blame for the Cultural Revolution is put on the "Gang of Four"— Mao's wife and three other hard-line officials, who are arrested. The 450-year-old Da Ming Men in the center of Tian'anmen Square is pulled down to make way for Mao's mausoleum. Leaders back Deng Xiaoping, who returns from disgrace to take power and launch a program of openness and economic reform. His own toleration for public criticism also turns out to be zero, however.

1989 The death of the moderate but disgraced official Hu Yaobang causes public displays of mourning in Tian'anmen Square, which turn into a mass occupation of the square protesting government corruption. Its hands initially tied by the presence of the Soviet Union's Mikhail Gorbachev on a state visit, the Party sends tanks into Tian'anmen Square, which is broadcast live on TV on the night of June 3. Estimates of the number of deaths vary wildly, but the number is thought to run to several hundred unarmed students and their supporters.

2001 Beijing is awarded the 2008 Summer Olympics.

2008 Beijing hosts the 2008 Summer Olympics as new monuments such as the Bird's Nest Stadium and the CCTV Tower are completed and many residents are displaced from old neighborhoods. Elsewhere in China, a powerful earthquake strikes Sichuan province and riots break out in Tibet.

2009 Beijing celebrates the 60th anniversary of the founding of the People's Republic of China. While much of the industrialized world falls into a recession, China continues to grow economically. Riots break out in China's northwest Xinjiang province.

TODAY China's economy continues to expand while the government still imposes certain limits on freedom and human rights. As to whether China can sustain high growth rates is questioned by many experts, yet it is becoming a larger industrial, cultural, and political force around the world.

Mandarin Language Guide

Pīnyīn Pronunciation

Letters in Pīnyīn mostly have the values any English speaker would expect, with the following exceptions:

c *ts* as in bi*ts*

q *ch* as in *ch*in, but much harder and more forward, made with tongue and teeth

r has no true equivalent in English, but the *r* of *r*eed is close, although the tip of the tongue should be near the top of the mouth, and the teeth together

x also has no true equivalent, but is nearest to the *sh* of *sh*eep, although the tongue should be parallel to the roof of the mouth and the teeth together

zh is a soft j, like the *dge* in ju*dge*

The vowels are pronounced roughly as follows:

a as in f*a*ther

e as in *e*rr (*leng* is pronounced as English "lung")

i is pronounced *ee* after most consonants, but after c, ch, r, s, sh, z, and zh is a buzz at the front of the mouth behind closed teeth

o as in s*o*ng

u as in t*oo*

ü is the purer, lips-pursed u of French t*u* and German *ü*. Confusingly, **u** after j, x, q, and y is always ü, but in these cases the accent over "ü" does not appear.

ai sounds like *eye*

ao as in *ou*ch

ei as in h*ay*

ia as in *ya*k

ian sounds like *yen*

iang sounds like *yang*

iu sounds like *you*

ou as in t*oe*

ua as in g*ua*va

ui sounds like *way*

uo sounds like *or,* but is more abrupt

Note that when two or more third-tone "â" sounds follow one another, they should all, except the last, be pronounced as second-tone "á"

Mandarin Bare Essentials
Greetings & Introductions

ENGLISH	PĪNYĪN	CHINESE
Hello	Nǐ hǎo	你好
How are you?	Nǐ hǎo ma?	你好吗？
Fine. And you?	Wǒ hěn hǎo. Nǐ ne?	我很好你呢？
I'm not too well/ Things aren't going well	Bù hǎo	不好
What is your name? (very polite)	Nín guì xìng?	您贵姓
My (family) name is	Wǒ xìng	我姓

I'm known as (family, then given name)	Wǒ jiào	我叫
I'm from [America]	Wǒ shì cóng [Měiguó] lái de	我是从美国来的
I'm [American]	Wǒ shì [Měiguó] rén	我是美国人
[Australian]	[Àodàlìyà]	澳大利亚
[British]	[Yīngguó]	英国
[Canadian]	[Jiānádà]	加拿大
[Irish]	[Àiěrlán]	爱尔兰
[a New Zealander]	[Xīnxīlán]	新西兰
Excuse me/I'm sorry	Duìbùqǐ	对不起
I don't understand	Wǒ tīng bù dǒng	我听不懂
Thank you	Xièxie nǐ	谢谢你
Correct (yes)	Duì	对
Not correct	Bú duì	不对
No, I don't want	Wǒ bú yào	我不要
Not acceptable	Bù xíng	不行

Basic Questions & Problems

ENGLISH	PĪNYĪN	CHINESE
Excuse me/I'd like to ask	Qǐng wènyíxià	请问一下
Where is . . . ?	. . . zài nǎr?	在哪儿？
How much is . . . ?	. . . duōshǎo qián?	多少钱？
. . . this one?	Zhèi/Zhè ge . . .	这个？
. . . that one?	Nèi/Nà ge . . .	那个？
Do you have . . . ?	Nǐ yǒu méi yǒu . . .	你有没有？
What time does/ is . . . ?	. . . jǐ diǎn?	几点？
What time is it now?	Xiànzài jǐ diǎn?	现在几点？
When is . . . ?	. . . shénme shíhou?	什么时候？
Why?	Wèishénme?	为什么？
Who?	Shéi?	谁？
Is that okay?	Xíng bù xíng?	行不行？
I'm feeling ill	Wǒ shēng bìng le	我生病

Travel

ENGLISH	PĪNYĪN	CHINESE
luxury (bus, hotel rooms)	háohuá	豪华
high speed (buses, expressways)	gāosù	高速
air-conditioned	kōngtiáo	空调
When's the last bus?	mòbānchē jǐdiǎn kāi?	末班车几点开

Numbers

Note that more complicated forms of numbers are often used on official documents and receipts to prevent fraud—see how easily 1 can be changed to 2, 3, or even 10. Familiar Arabic numerals appear on bank notes, most signs, taxi meters, and other places. Be particularly careful with "four" and "ten," which sound very alike in many regions—hold up fingers to make sure. Note, too, that yī, meaning "one," tends to change its tone all the time depending on what it precedes. Don't worry about this—once you've started talking about money, almost any kind of squeak for "one" will do. Finally note that "two" alters when being used with expressions of quantity.

ENGLISH	PĪNYĪN	CHINESE
zero	líng	零
one	yī	一
two	èr	二
two (of them)	liǎng ge	两个
three	sān	三
four	sì	四
five	wǔ	五
six	liù	六
seven	qī	七
eight	bā	八
nine	jiǔ	九
10	shí	十
11	shí yī	十一
12	shí èr	十二
21	èr shí yī	二十一
22	èr shí èr	二十二
51	wǔ shí yī	五十一
100	yì bǎi	一百
101	yì bǎi líng yī	一百零一
110	yì bǎi yī (shí)	一百一十
111	yì bǎi yī shí yī	一百一十一
1,000	yì qiān	一千
1,500	yì qiān wǔ (bǎi)	一千五百
5,678	wǔ qiān liù bǎi qī shí bā	五千六百七十八
10,000	yí wàn	一万

Money

ENGLISH	PĪNYĪN	CHINESE
¥1	yí kuài qián	一块钱
¥2	liǎng kuài qián	两块钱
¥0.30	sān máo qián	三毛钱
¥5.05	wǔ kuài líng wǔ fēn	五块零五分
¥5.50	wǔ kuài wǔ	五块五
¥550	wǔ bǎi wǔ shí kuài	五百五十块
¥5,500	wǔ qiān wǔ bǎi kuài	五千五百块
small change	língqián	零钱

Banking & Shopping

ENGLISH	PĪNYĪN	CHINESE
I want to change money (foreign exchange)	Wǒ xiǎng huàn qián	我想换钱
credit card	xìnyòng kǎ	信用卡
traveler's check	lǚxíng zhīpiào	旅行支票
department store	bǎihuò shāngdiàn or gòuwù zhōngxīn	百货商店 购物中心

ENGLISH	PĪNYĪN	CHINESE
convenience store	xiǎomàibù	小卖部
market	shìchǎng	市场
May I have a look?	Wǒ kànyíxia, hǎo ma?	我看一下，好吗？
I want to buy	Wǒ xiǎng mǎi	我想买
How many do you want?	Nǐ yào jǐ ge?	你要几个？
two of them	liǎng ge	两个
three of them	sān ge	三个
1 kilo (2¼ lb.)	yì gōngjīn	一公斤
half a kilo	yì jīn or bàn gōngjīn	一斤 公斤
1 meter (3¼ ft.)	yì mǐ	一米
Too expensive!	Tài guì le!	太贵了！
Do you have change?	Yǒu língqián ma?	有零钱吗？

Time

ENGLISH	PĪNYĪN	CHINESE
morning	shàngwǔ	上午
afternoon	xiàwǔ	下午
evening	wǎnshang	晚上
8:20am	shàngwǔ bā diǎn èr shí fēn	上午八点二十分
9:30am	shàngwǔ jiǔ diǎn bàn	上午九点半
noon	zhōngwǔ	中午
4:15pm	xiàwǔ sì diǎn yí kè	下午四点一刻
midnight	wǔ yè	午夜
1 hour	yí ge xiǎoshí	一个小时
8 hours	bā ge xiǎoshí	八个小时
today	jīntiān	今天
yesterday	zuótiān	昨天
tomorrow	míngtiān	明天
Monday	Xīngqī yī	星期一
Tuesday	Xīngqī èr	星期二
Wednesday	Xīngqī sān	星期三
Thursday	Xīngqī sì	星期四
Friday	Xīngqī wǔ	星期五
Saturday	Xīngqī liù	星期六
Sunday	Xīngqī tiān	星期天

Transport

ENGLISH	PĪNYĪN	CHINESE
I want to go to . . .	Wǒ xiǎng qù . . .	我想去
plane	fēijī	飞机
train	huǒchē	火车
bus	gōnggòng qìchē	公共汽车
long-distance bus	chángtú qìchē	长途汽车
taxi	chūzū chē	出租车
airport	fēijīchǎng	飞机场
stop or station (bus or train)	zhàn	站
(plane/train/bus) ticket	piào	票

Navigation

ENGLISH	PĪNYĪN	CHINESE
North	Běi	北
South	Nán	南
East	Dōng	东
West	Xī	西
Turn left	zuǒ guǎi	左拐
Turn right	yòu guǎi	右拐
Go straight on	yìzhí zǒu	一直走
crossroads	shízì lùkǒu	十字路口
10 kilometers	shí gōnglǐ	十公里
I'm lost	Wǒ diū le	我丢了

Hotel

ENGLISH	PĪNYĪN	CHINESE
How many days?	Zhù jǐ tiān?	住几天?
standard room (twin or double with private bathroom)	biāozhǔn jiān	标准间
passport	hùzhào	护照
deposit	yājīn	押金
I want to check out	Wǒ tuì fáng	我退房

Restaurant

ENGLISH	PĪNYĪN	CHINESE
How many people?	Jǐ wèi?	几位?
waiter/waitress	fúwùyuán	服务员
menu	càidān	菜单
I'm vegetarian	Wǒ shì chī sù de	我是吃素的
Don't add MSG	qǐng bù fàng wèijīng	请不放味精
Do you have . . . ?	Yǒu méi yǒu . . . ?	有没有?
Please bring a portion of . . .	Qǐng lái yí fènr . . .	请来一份儿
I'm full	wǒ chībǎo le	我吃饱了
beer	píjiǔ	啤酒
coffee	kāfēi	咖啡
mineral water	kuàngquán shuǐ	矿泉水
tea	cháshuǐ	茶水
Bill, please	jiézhàng	结帐

Beijing **Menu Reader**

One of the best things about any visit to China is the food, at least for the independent traveler. Tour groups are often treated to a relentless series of cheap, bland dishes designed to cause no complaints and to keep the costs down for the Chinese operator, so do everything you can to escape and order some of the specialties we describe for you in chapter 5. Here they are again, in alphabetical order and with characters you can show to the waitress.

Widely available dishes and snacks are grouped in the first list; you can order most of them in any mainstream or *jiachang cai* ("homestyle") restaurant. Some dishes recommended in this guidebook's reviews of individual restaurants are commonly available enough to be on this first list. Note that some of the specialty dishes in the second list are only available in the restaurants reviewed, or in restaurants offering a particular region's cuisine.

Supplement these lists with the bilingual menu from your local Chinese restaurant at home. The characters will not be quite the same as those used in Beijing (more similar to those used in Hong Kong and Macau), but they will be understood. Don't expect the dishes to be the same, however. Expect them to be *better*.

Any mainstream nonspecialty restaurant can and will make any common Chinese dish, whether it's on the menu or not. But don't expect Beijing cooks to manage the subtler flavors of Cantonese cooking, for instance, unless the restaurant advertises itself as a southern-food specialist.

A surprising number of restaurants now have English menus. In the past, this was a warning of inflated prices, but now an English menu is often used to brand a restaurant as "classy" in the eyes of the locals.

Dishes often arrive in haphazard order, but menus generally open with *liang cai* (cold dishes). Except in top-class Sino-foreign joint-venture restaurants, you are strongly advised to avoid these for hygiene reasons. The restaurant's specialties also come early in the menu: They have significantly higher prices and if you dither, the waitress will recommend them, saying, "I hear this one's good." Waitresses always recommend ¥180 dishes, never ¥8 ones. Some of these dishes may occasionally be made from creatures you would regard as pets or zoo creatures (or best in the wild), and parts of them you may consider inedible or odd, like swallow saliva (the main ingredient of bird's-nest soup, a rather bland Cantonese delicacy).

Main dishes come next; various meats and fish are followed by vegetables and *doufu* (tofu). Drinks come at the end. You'll rarely find desserts outside of restaurants that largely cater to foreigners. A few watermelon slices may appear, but it's best to forgo them.

Soup is usually eaten last. Outside Guangdong Province, Hong Kong, and Macau, rice also usually arrives at the end; if you want it with your meal, you must ask (point to the characters for rice, below, when the first dish arrives).

There is no tipping. Tea, chopsticks, and napkins should be free (although if a wrapped packet of tissues arrives you may pay a small fee); service charges do not exist outside of major hotels; and there are no cover charges or taxes. If asked what tea you would like, know that you are going to receive something above average and will be charged for it. (Exercise caution! Some varieties cost more than the meal.)

Most Chinese dishes are not designed to be eaten solo, but if you do find yourself on your own, ask for small portions *(xiao pan)*, usually about 70% of the size of a full dish and about 70% of the price. This allows you to sample the menu properly without too much waste.

Widely Available Dishes & Snacks

PĪNYĪN	ENGLISH	CHINESE
babao zhou	rice porridge with nuts and berries	八宝粥
bǎnli shāo chìzhōng	soy chicken wings with chestnuts	板栗烧翅中

PĪNYĪN	ENGLISH	CHINESE
bāozi	stuffed steamed buns	包子
bīngqílín	ice cream	冰淇淋
chǎo fàn	fried rice	炒饭
chǎo miàn	fried noodles	炒面
cōng bào niúròu	quick-fried beef and onions	葱爆牛肉
dāndān miàn	noodles in spicy broth	担担面
diǎnxin	dim sum (snacks)	点心
dì sān xiān	braised eggplant with potatoes and spicy green peppers	地三鲜
gānbiān sìjìdòu	sautéed string beans	干煸四季豆
gōngbào jīdīng	spicy diced chicken with cashews	宫爆鸡丁
guōtiē	fried dumplings/ potstickers	锅贴
hóngshāo fǔzhú	braised tofu	红烧腐竹
hóngshāo huángyú	braised yellow fish	红烧黄鱼
huíguō ròu	twice-cooked pork	回锅肉
huǒguō	hot pot	火锅
jiānbing	large crepe folded around fried dough with plum and hot sauces	煎饼
jiǎozi	dumplings/Chinese ravioli	饺子
jīngjiàng ròu sī	shredded pork in soya sauce	京酱肉丝
mápó dòufu	spicy tofu with chopped meat	麻婆豆腐
miàntiáo	noodles	面条
mǐfàn	rice	米饭
mù xū ròu	sliced pork with fungus (mushu pork)	木须肉
niúròu miàn	beef noodles	牛肉面
ròu chuàn	kebabs/kabobs	肉串
sānxiān	"three flavors" (usually prawn, mushroom, pork)	三鲜
shuǐjiǎo	boiled dumplings	水饺
suānlà báicài	hot and sour cabbage	酸辣白菜
suānlà tāng	hot and sour soup	酸辣汤
sù miàn	vegetarian noodles	素面
sù shíjǐn	mixed vegetables	素什锦
tángcù lǐjí	sweet-and-sour pork tenderloin	糖醋里脊
tǔdòu dùn niúròu	stewed beef and potato	土豆炖牛肉
xiàn bǐng	pork- or vegetable- stuffed fried pancake	馅饼
xīhóngshì chǎo jīdàn	tomatoes with eggs	西红柿炒鸡蛋

PĪNYĪN	ENGLISH	CHINESE
yángròu chuàn	barbecued lamb skewers with ground cumin and chili powder	羊肉串
yóutiáo	fried salty donut	油条
yúxiāng qiézi	eggplant in garlic sauce	鱼香茄子
yúxiāng ròu sī	shredded pork in garlic sauce	鱼香肉丝
zhēngjiǎo	steamed dumplings	蒸饺
zhōu	rice porridge	粥

Specialty Dishes Recommended in Restaurant Reviews

PĪNYĪN	ENGLISH	CHINESE
bābǎo làjiàng	gingko, nuts, and pork in sweet chili sauce	八宝辣酱
bōluó fàn	pineapple rice	菠萝饭
cháshùgū bāo lǎojī	chicken with tea-mushroom soup	茶树菇煲老鸡
chénpí lǎoyā shānzhēn bāo	duck, mandarin peel, and mushroom potage	陈皮老鸭山珍煲
cuìpí qiézi	sweet and sour battered eggplant	脆皮茄子
cùngū shāo	deep-fried pork with medicinal herbs	寸骨烧
Dǎizú xiāngmáocǎo kǎo yú	Dǎi grilled lemon grass fish	傣族香茅草烤鱼
dà lāpí	cold noodles in sesame and vinegar sauce	大拉皮
dà pán jī	diced chicken and noodles in tomato sauce	大盘鸡
Dōngběi fēngwèi dàpái	northeast-style braised ribs	东北风味大排
Dōngpō ròu	braised fatty pork in small clay pot	东坡肉
é'gān juǎn	gooseliver rolls with hoisin sauce	鹅肝卷
gǒubùlǐ bāozi	pork-stuffed bread dumplings	狗不里包子
guōbā ròu piān	pork with crispy fried rice	锅巴肉片
guòqiáo mǐxiàn	crossing-the-bridge rice noodles	过桥米线
huángdì sǔn shāo wánzi	Imperial bamboo shoots and vegetarian meatballs	皇帝笋烧丸子
huángqiáo ròu sūbǐng	shredded-pork rolls	黄桥肉酥饼
huíxiāng dòu	aniseed-flavored beans	茴香豆
jiāoliū wánzi	crisp-fried pork balls	焦熘丸子
jīngjiàng ròusī	shredded pork with green onion rolled in tofu skin	京酱肉丝

PĪNYĪN	ENGLISH	CHINESE
jīnpái tiáoliào	"gold label" sesame sauce (for Mongolian hot pot)	金牌调料
jīròu sèlā	deep-fried chicken pieces with herb dipping sauce	鸡肉色拉
jiǔxiāng yúgān	dried fish in wine sauce	酒香鱼干
juébā chǎo làròu	bacon stir-fried with brake leaves	蕨粑炒腊肉
kǎo yángròu	roast mutton	烤羊肉
làbā cù	garlic-infused vinegar	腊八醋
láncài sìjìdòu	green beans stir-fried with salty vegetable	榄菜四季豆
lǎogānmā shāojī	spicy diced chicken with bamboo and ginger	老干妈烧鸡
làròu dòuyá juǎnbǐng	spicy bacon and bean sprouts in pancakes	腊肉豆芽卷饼
làwèi huájī bāozǎi fàn	chicken and sweet sausage on rice in clay pot	腊味滑鸡煲仔饭
liángbàn zǐ lúsǔn	purple asparagus salad	凉拌紫芦笋
luóbo sī sūbǐng	shredded-turnip shortcake	萝卜丝酥饼
málà lóngxiā	spicy crayfish	麻辣龙虾
málà tiánluó	field snails stewed in chili and Sichuān pepper	麻辣田螺
mǎtí niúliǔ	stir-fried beef with broccoli, water chestnuts, and tofu rolls	马蹄牛柳
mìzhì zhǐbāo lúyú	paper-wrapped perch and onions on sizzling iron plate	秘制纸包鲈鱼
náng bāo ròu	lamb and vegetable stew served on flat wheat bread	馕包肉
nánrǔ kòuròu	braised pork in red fermented bean curd gravy	南乳扣肉
niúròu wán shuǐjiǎo	beef ball dumplings	牛肉丸水饺
nóngjiā shāo jiān jī	spicy sautéed chicken fillet	农家烧煎鸡
nóngjiā xiǎochǎo	soybeans, green onion, Chinese chives, and green pepper in a clay pot	农家小炒
qiáo miàn māo ěrduo	"cat's ear" buckwheat pasta with chopped meat	荞面猫耳朵
ròudīng báicài xiànbǐng	meat cabbage pie	肉丁白菜馅饼
rúyì hǎitái juǎn	vegetarian sushi rolls	如意海苔卷

PĪNYĪN	ENGLISH	CHINESE
sānxiān làohé	seafood and garlic chive buns	三鲜烙合
sè shāo niúròu	foil-wrapped beef marinated in mountain herbs	色烧牛肉
shāchá niúròu	beef sautéed with Taiwanese BBQ sauce	沙茶牛肉
shānyao gēng	yam broth with mushrooms	山药羹
shānyao húlu	red bean rolls with mountain herbs	山药葫芦
shēngjiān bāozi	pork-stuffed fried bread dumplings	生煎包子
shǒuzhuā fàn	Uighur-style rice with carrot and mutton	手抓饭
shǒuzhuā yáng pái	lamb chops roasted with cumin and chili	手抓羊排
sān bēi jī	chicken reduced in rice wine, sesame oil, and soy sauce	三杯鸡
shuǐzhǔ yú	boiled fish in spicy broth with numbing peppercorns	水煮鱼
suànxiāng jīchì	garlic paper-wrapped chicken wings	蒜香鸡翅
sǔngān lǎoyā bāo	stewed duck with dried bamboo shoots	笋干老鸭煲
Táiwān dòufu bāo	Taiwanese tofu and vegetables clay pot	台湾豆腐煲
tiānfú shāokǎo yángtuǐ	roasted leg of mutton with cumin and chili powder	天福烧烤羊腿
tiēbǐngzi	corn pancakes cooked on a griddle	贴饼子
tǔdòu qiú	deep-fried potato balls with chili sauce	土豆球
tǔtāng shícài	clear soup with seasonal leafy greens	土汤时菜
xiāngcǎo cuìlà yú	whole fried fish with hot peppers and lemon grass	香草脆辣鱼
xiǎolóng bāozi	pork-stuffed steamed bread dumplings	小笼包子
Xībèi dà bàncài	Xībèi salad	西贝大拌菜
xièfěn dòufu	crab meat tofu	蟹粉豆腐
xièsānxiān shuǐjiǎo	boiled crab dumplings with shrimp and mushrooms	蟹三鲜水饺
yángròu chuàn	spicy mutton skewers with cumin	羊肉串
yángyóu má dòufu	mashed soybean with lamb oil	羊油麻豆腐

PĪNYĪN	ENGLISH	CHINESE
yán jú xiā	shrimp skewers in rock salt	盐局虾
yè niúròu juǎn	grilled la lop leaf beef	叶牛肉卷
yì bǎ zhuā	fried wheat cakes	一把抓
yóumiàn wōwo	steamed oatmeal noodles	莜面窝窝
yóutiáo niúròu	sliced beef with fried dough in savory sauce	油条牛肉
zhá guàncháng	taro chips with garlic sauce	炸灌肠
zhāngchá yā	crispy smoked duck with plum sauce	樟茶鸭
zhá qiéhé	pork-stuffed deep-fried eggplant	炸茄合
zhēnzhū nǎichá	pearl milk tea	珍珠奶茶
zhǐbāo lúyú	paper-wrapped perch in sweet sauce	纸包鲈鱼
zhījīcǎo kǎo niúpái	lotus leaf–wrapped roast beef with mountain herbs	枳机草烤牛排
zhūròu báicài bāozi	steamed bun stuffed with pork and cabbage	猪肉白菜包子
zhúsūn qìguō jī	mushroom and mountain herbs chicken soup	竹荪气锅鸡
zhútǒng jī	chicken soup in bamboo vessel	竹筒鸡
zhútǒng páigǔ	spicy stewed pork with mint	竹筒排骨
zhútǒng zhūròu	steamed pork with coriander	竹筒猪肉
zuì jī	chicken marinated in rice wine	醉鸡
zuì xiā	live shrimp in wine	醉虾

Recommended **Books**

The best single-volume introduction to the people of China and their world is **Jonathan D. Spence**'s *The Search for Modern China* (Norton 1990). Spence is a noted historian who currently teaches at Yale University. The book begins with the glory of the Ming dynasty and ends with the opening of China and the tensions in the final decades of the 20th century. It is an incredibly vivid and engaging read.

Old Beijing can now only be found in literature. The origins of many Western fantasies of the capital, then called Khanbalik, lie in the ghost-written work of **Marco Polo**, *The Travels of Marco Polo*. Dover Publications' two-volume reprint (1993) of the Yule-Cordier edition is a splendid read (although only part of Polo's time was spent in Beijing) because of its entertaining introduction and footnotes by famous explorers attempting to follow his route. **Ray Huang**'s ironically titled *1587: A Year of No Significance* (Yale University Press, 1982) is an account of the Ming dynasty in decline;

written in the first person, it paints a compelling picture of the well-intentioned Wànlì emperor trapped by a vast, impersonal bureaucracy. **Lord Macartney**'s *An Embassy to China* (J. L. Cranmer-Byng [ed.], Longman, 1962) gives a detailed account of Qing China and particularly Beijing at the end of the 18th century. This should be compulsory reading for modern businesspeople, as it prefigures WTO negotiations and the expectations of what will arise from them. Macartney's prediction that the Chinese would all soon be using forks and spoons is particularly relevant. **Hugh Trevor-Roper**'s *Hermit of Peking* (Eland Press, 1976), part history, part detective story, uncovers the life of Sir Edmund Backhouse, resident of Beijing from the end of the Qing dynasty into the Republic. He knew everyone in the city at the beginning of the century, and deceived them all, along with a generation of China scholars, with his fake diary of a Manchu official at the time of the Boxer Rebellion. A serviceable translated bilingual edition of **Lao She**'s *Teahouse* (Chinese University Press, 2004) succinctly captures the flavor of life in Beijing during the first half of the 20th century. The helplessness of the characters in the face of political movements is both moving and prophetic. **John Blofeld**'s *City of Lingering Splendour: A Frank Account of Old Peking's Exotic Pleasures* (Shambala, 1961) describes the seamier side of Beijing in the 1930s, by someone who took frank enjoyment in its pleasures, including adventures in "the lanes of flowers and willows"—the Qian Men brothel quarter. **Ann Bridge,** the wife of a British diplomat in Beijing, wrote novels of life in the capital's Legation Quarter in the 1930s (cocktail parties, horse racing, problems with servants, love affairs—spicy stuff in its day, and best-selling, if now largely forgotten). *Peking Picnic* (Chatto and Windus, 1932; reprinted Virago, 1989) features a disastrous trip to the outlying temples of Tánzhè Sì and Jiètái Sì (but one well worth undertaking yourself). *The Ginger Griffin* (Chatto and Windus, 1934; reprinted by Oxford University Press, 1985) offers the adventures of a young woman newly arrived in the city who attends the horse races, and has a happier ending.

Dr. Li Zhisui was the personal physician of Mao Zedong. His frank and vivid novel *The Private Life of Chairman Mao* (Random House, 1994) reveals surprising details about the sexual politics of Mao's court. Perhaps the best example of the "hooligan literature" of the late 1980s is *Please Don't Call Me Human* (No Exit Press, 2000), by **Wáng Shuò**. There's little plot to speak of, but it's a devastating and surreal parody of Chinese nationalism. *Black Hands of Beijing* (John Wiley, Inc., 1993), by **George Black and Robin Munro,** is the most balanced and least hysterical account of the Tian'anmen protests of 1989, putting them in the context of other, better-planned movements for social change, all of which suffered in the fallout from the chaotic student demonstrations and their bloody suppression. *One Billion Customers: Lessons from the Front Lines of Doing Business in China* (Free Press, 2005) is a well-researched and personal account of how business in China is conducted—with a lot of subterfuge and plenty of headaches. The author is **James McGregor,** who has lived in China for more than 2 decades and was bureau chief for The *Wall Street Journal* during the Tia'nanmen Massacre, chief executive of Dow Jones through the '90s, and a venture capitalist during China's dot.com boom. An excellent autobiography that gives an insightful perspective on modern China is **Peter Hessler**'s *River Town* (Harper, 2001). The book documents Hessler's two-year Peace Corps stint as a college teacher in rural China. Hessler went on to become the correspondent for *The New Yorker* in Beijing. His encounters in China are further documented in his second book, *Oracle Bones: A Journey Between China's Past and Present* (Harper, 2006). This book is also an excellent read, with well-researched historical stories of various Chinese scholars and everyday people thrown in for good measure. The author of this book, **Jen Lin-Liu,** has published a memoir of her experiences learning how to cook in China, called *Serve the People: A Stir-Fried Journey Through China.* Other excellent books include **Michael Meyer**'s *The Last Days of Old Beijing* and **Leslie Chang**'s *Factory Girls.*

Chris Elder's *Old Peking: City of the Ruler of the World* (Oxford University Press, 1997) is a compendium of comments on the city from a wide range of literary and historical sources, sorted by topic. For those intent on digging out the last remains of the capital's ancient architecture, **Susan Naquin**'s magisterial *Peking Temples and City Life, 1400–1900* (University of California Press, 2000) gives a scholarly yet readable background to many buildings now open to the public and many now long vanished. **Frances Wood**'s *Forbidden City* (British Museum Press, 2005) is a short and thoroughly entertaining introduction to Beijing's main attraction.

Toll-Free Numbers & Websites

Airlines

AIR CANADA
☎ 888/247-2262 in North America
☎ 010/6468-2001 in China
www.aircanada.com

AIR CHINA
☎ 010/6466-1697 in China
www.airchina.com.cn

AIR FRANCE
☎ 800/237-2747 in the U.S.
☎ 4008/808-808 in China
www.airfrance.com

AIR MACAU
☎ 010/6515-9398 in China
http://bj.airmacau.com.cn

ALL NIPPON AIRWAYS
☎ 800/235-9262 in North America
☎ 010/6590-9177 in China
www.anaskyweb.com/us/e

BANGKOK AIRWAYS
☎ 866/BANGKOK in North America
☎ 010/6430-1517 in China
www.bangkokair.com

BRITISH AIRWAYS
☎ 0870/850-9850 in the U.K.
☎ 400/650-0073 in China
www.britishairways.com

CATHAY PACIFIC
☎ 800/233-2742 in the U.S.
☎ 010/800852-1888 in China
www.cathaypacific.com

CONTINENTAL AIRLINES
☎ 800/523-3273 in the U.S. & Mexico
☎ 010/8527-6696 in China
www.continental.com

DRAGON AIRLINES
☎ 010/6518-2533 in China
www.dragonair.com

JAPAN AIRLINES
☎ 800/525-3663 in North America
☎ 400/888-0808 in China
www.jal.com

KLM ROYAL DUTCH AIRLINES
See Northwest Airlines.

KOREAN AIR
☎ 800/438-5000 in North America
☎ 010/8453-8421 in China
www.koreanair.com

LUFTHANSA
☎ 800/399-5838 in the U.S.
☎ 010/6468-8838 in China
www.lufthansa.com

MALAYSIA AIRLINES
☎ 010/6505-2681 in China
www.malaysiaairlines.com

NORTHWEST AIRLINES
☎ 800/225-2525 in the U.S.
☎ 400/814-0081 in China
www.nwa.com

QANTAS AIRLINES
☎ (02) 9691-3636 in Australia
☎ 010/6567-9006 in China
www.qantas.com

SCANDINAVIAN AIRLINES
☎ 800/221-2350 in the U.S.
☎ 010/8527-6100 in China
www.flysas.com

THAI AIRWAYS INTERNATIONAL
☎ 010/8515-0088 in China
www.thaiair.com

UNITED AIRLINES
☎ 800/864-8331 in the U.S.
☎ 010/8468-6666 in China
www.united.com

Index

See also Accommodations and Restaurant indexes, below.

Photo **Credits**

Notes